Rosema

CAIQUES

dona

ACKNOWLEDGEMENTS

The author acknowledges with thanks permission to use the following photographs from Thomas Brosset (photo 18), Lars Lepperhoff (photos 19, 20, 24, 25) and Robin Restall (photo 27).

All other photographs are by the author.

ISBN 80-7322-044-X

Contents

Introduction

In appearance and behaviour Caiques are among the most distinctive of parrots. Their personality is also unique. No other parrot has the same combination of characteristics: fearless, inquisitive and playful with a huge ego and a strong willpower. Their appeal is immediate: the upright stance, cheeky manner and unusual colour scheme.

No wonder their popularity has rocketed with breeders and with companion parrot owners in recent years! The leading avicultural bookseller in the UK told me that he was repeatedly being asked for a book on caiques. So here it is!

All the information in this book relates specifically to caiques, except that on health care, which applies to all parrots. There can be nothing more irritating to buy a book that purports to be on a specific subject only to find that most of the information has a much more general application!

Chapter 1

What is a Caique?

Caiques are small parrots of the genus *Pionites*. Two species, the Black-headed and the White-bellied, are recognised. However, research using DNA techniques will probably show that they are all sub-species of one species.

First of all, how does one pronounce the word caique? In the UK it tends to be pronounced like the word cake while, in the USA these little parrots are called *kyeeks*. The latter pronunciation is probably more accurate – and perhaps the word should be written as *caique* to make this clear. No matter! Their appeal is not in doubt. These bouncing, sharp-eyed and alert little parrots conceal a personality as big as a macaw's. They have no idea that they are small. In an antagonistic encounter they would take on an Amazon, yet they are so sociable that, needing a companion, they would cuddle up to a cockatoo.

Caiques are bundles of fun who love to play and to explore. Their fascinating behaviour and their small size makes them almost ideal subjects for the home. If they have a fault, it is their shrill calls. Caiques measure only 23cm (9in) and weigh approximately 160g. The two species are the Black-headed and the White-bellied – Caiques to aviculturists but usually referred to as "parrots" in field guides.

Black-headed Caique
(Pionites melanocephala melanocephala)

The top of the head, from forehead to nape, is black. The lores and a very narrow line below the eye are green, with a few white feathers below the green ones. The throat and cheeks are yellow, merging into orange on the nape and hind neck. The entire upperparts (wings, back, rump and tail) are mid-green and the underparts, from upper breast to lower abdomen are white, although the feathers are not always snowy! The orange-yellow under tail coverts and orange thighs show yellow on the margins of some feathers. The primaries and primary coverts are black, with the outer webs deep blue, edged with green. The iris has an inner ring of black or grey and an outer one of bright ruby-red. The beak is black. The bare skin surrounding the eye is grey, as is the cere, and the feet are darker grey.

Geographical variations

I am indebted to Robin Restall, research associate at the Phelps Museum in Caracas, for examining and photographing skins of the nominate race from different areas of Venezuela. These can be seen in the photograph on the last colour page. He commented as follows:

"On the left, the first four specimens are from the Delta Amacuro – the great wadge of mangrove swamp that is the mouth of the Orinoco river. These birds are a rich orange. The rest of that row and the entire middle row are all from the state of Bolivar, the round bulge of Venezuela south of the Orinoco that adjoins Guyana. These birds are a slightly richer orange than those from the Delta. Most noticeable is the contrast with the birds on the right in this middle row, which are especially reddish--orange. They are from the Cuyuni valley. The Cuyuni is the only river in Venezuela that runs out of the country (and into Guyana) instead of into the Orinoco.

The birds in the bottom row are all from the Upper Orinoco, the Amazonas state. These birds are more yellow than orange, though nothing like the clean lemon yellow of *pallida*. In my opinion, this group is sufficiently distinct to warrant specific separation from *melanocephala*. In the area where these birds are found canopy species have seldom been collected. In the old days the only way to get to this country was by a small boat up the Orinoco. It was next to impossible to get there in the rainy season, that is, when all the birds are there, breeding. Then the explorers were obsessed with getting to Mount Neblina on the Brazilian border."

Immature Black-headed Caiques have the underparts yellowish-white or pale buff but the colour varies in individuals. In some birds the white feathers are margined with yellow and the occasional young bird has the underparts strongly suffused with dull orange. The rest of the plumage is slightly paler throughout. There might be a blue tinge to the green on the wings. The bill is grey, and the iris brown, gradually changing to reddish--brown. The naked skin surrounding the eye and on the cere is pinkish-grey (darker grey in adults).

Pallid Caique
(P. m. pallida)

This is not a well-defined sub-species. The lemon yellow thighs, flanks and under tail coverts are said to distinguish it from the nominate race – but see above, regarding the range of shades of orange found in the nominate race which probably intergrades with *pallida*. In reality, however, a mixture of yellow and orange is found on the thighs of many adult Black-headed Caiques.

White-bellied Caique
(Pionites leucogaster leucogaster)

The black head of the better-known caique is replaced by orange – extending from the forehead to the lower part of the nape.

Lores, cheeks and throat are yellow. Note the thigh colour: it is green in the nominate race which is rare in captivity. The beak is whitish. In all the birds of the nominate race that I have seen, the pink skin surrounding the eyes and cere is more vivid than in *xanthomeria*, the feet are pink and the nails are white. In other words, remove the melanin from a Black-headed Caique and this is what you get! In *xanthomeria* the colours of the soft parts and toenails are variable. The outer iris ring is not such a bright red as in the Black-headed Caique.

Yellow-thighed Caique
(P. l. xanthomeria)

It differs from the nominate race in having the thighs and flanks yellow instead of green. To my eyes, the pink-footed form of the Yellow-thighed Caique is the most beautiful of the genus known in Europe, while those with black feet somehow look incongruous as the black feet contrast oddly with the light beak. But by any standards they are beautiful birds!

The colour of the feet varies in individuals from black, through grey to flesh colour. Birds with grey feet have grey nails; those with flesh-coloured feet might also lack pigment in the nails, which are white, while others have pale grey nails. In the eye of the White--bellied Caique, the inner ring is usually grey – not black. The naked skin around the eye is white in some individuals, grey in others.

According to Sick (1993), in birds from the upper Amazon region, the bare skin around the eye is blackish. I have a slide of a young bird in my care photographed in 1974. The colours on the slide are very strong and they show the skin around the eye and the feet as being solid jet black, also the sides of the upper mandible as black. When I received this bird, on loan from George Smith, I made the note: "Black eye rings, black marks on upper mandible." I cannot recall seeing another *xanthomeria* in which the soft parts were so heavily pigmented.

Immature birds differ from adults in having the underparts yellowish-white or buff and, in some individuals, the wings tinged with blue. The skin surrounding the eye is pinkish in newly fledged young. The most striking difference is that the crown is irregularly marked with black feathers. This has led uninformed people to believe that they are hybrids between the Black-headed Caique and *leucogaster*. Young birds have the beak, legs, feet and exposed skin streaked with black, which is gradually lost during the first year, except in the case of those individuals that retain black legs into adulthood. Most of the black marks on the head are lost at the first moult, by about ten months, but in young with more extensive black markings, some black feathers might be retained after the first moult.

In young chicks the beak is flesh-coloured, but gradually acquires pigment and a patchy greyish appearance by the time of fledging. This grey tinge is apparent until the young birds reach about ten months. The dark iris of newly fledged young is retained for many months, changing gradually to adult colour at over one year of age.

Yellow-tailed Caique
(P. l. xanthurus)

This is a very striking bird, distinguished from *xanthomeria* by the entirely yellow tail. Its plumage is paler throughout. I think this is the most beautiful member of the genus – but most aviculturists will never have the opportunity to judge. I have seen this form only in a private collection in Brazil. The single individual (illustrated) had the feet flesh-coloured, the nails whitish and the bare skin surrounding the eye whitish with a pink tinge. I have been told that the Yellow-tailed Caique was kept in a private collection in Switzerland some years ago.

Immature birds

It is not unusual for immature plumage in parrots to show atavistic features and, in this case, is an indication of how closely the two forms are related. It is well known that newly fledged *leucogaster* have black feathers on the head. Further evidence is found in the appearance of newly fledged Black-headed Caiques, some of which tend towards *leucogaster*. As an example, one young Pallid Caique had the beak and feet entirely black, while its sibling had a light-coloured bill and toenails and flesh-pink toes.

Mutations

A lutino was apparently imported into England many years ago. No other mutations are known.

Plumage

In recent years the plumage of various parrot species has been studied under ultraviolet light, revealing unexpected colours. These are the colours that birds see. Apparently, under ultra-violet light the orange nape feathers of the Black-headed Caique and the orange head and nape of the White-bellied fluoresce a bright yellow while, strangely, the yellow feathers of the throat appear dark.

Behaviour

Behaviourally caiques are among the most fascinating of parrots. They display and vocalise loudly in a penetrating voice at the slightest provocation. The display is not unlike that of some *Pyrrhura* conures, but more exaggerated. Caiques lean forward on the perch and sway their bodies in a circular motion, sometimes opening and vibrating the wings at great speed so that they appear a blur. When excited they dilate their pupils so that they blaze red-orange.

Caiques do not move, act or vocalize like other short-tailed neotropical parrots. After studying neotropical parrots for most of my life, I believe that behaviourally they are nearest to the *Pyrrhura* conures and Hawk-headed Parrots *(Deroptyus accipitrinus)*, with their swaying threat display, their love of sleeping in hole and their heightened sense of curiosity. They often swagger about, seemingly afraid of nothing or no one. The term "larger than life" definitely applies to these handsome little parrots.

It has been suggested that their scientific name, *Pionites*, means like *Pionus*, another group of small neotropical parrots. However, in behaviour and appearance they do not resemble *Pionus* except for their plump, short-tailed silhouettes. The way they swagger along the perch, with tail flared, in display, is common to many neotropical parrots.

Caiques have a highly distinctive manner of locomotion with movements that are quick and precise. On the ground they have the ability to move very fast and, when excited, they hop in a way that is quite unlike any other parrot, and with a peculiarly upright stance. Among branches they climb with speed (not at the measured pace of an Amazon, for example) and with the agility of a monkey.

Caiques are, along with the lories, the most playful of all parrots. I have seen a caique hanging from the aviary roof by one foot and swinging its mate with the other, like a trapeze artiste! Every item encountered is either a potential toy or perhaps a rubbing post. Although they are not from the same continent and are in no way related, lories have quite a lot in common with caiques in their quick movements, playful behaviour, calculated aggression towards other birds and their extremely affectionate natures. Both groups of parrots share a habit that can cause heart palpitations in the carer if he or she is unaware of it. They like to lie on their backs and will sometimes do so, on the cage or aviary floor, feet in the air but quite still, as though they have departed this world! Chicks in the brooder might do the same thing!

Voice

Caiques make distinctive sounds, consisting of metallic clinks and yaps and other penetrating noises, including a shrill whistling shriek that might be repeated (too) often. A louder shriek is used to warn of danger. Before buying a caique, the prospective owner should listen to these sounds to ensure that he can tolerate them at close range. It is not accurate to state that caiques are quiet parrots.

In Guyana, E. McLoughlin made some interesting observations on the vocalisations of wild caiques:

> Commonly heard rather than seen, its most specific call seemed to be uttered when slightly disturbed. This call, an arresting, often repeated "keeya-keeya", resembled closely the corresponding call of *D. accipitrinus*. The call of *P. melanocephala* is frequently prefixed by a characteristic, fairly long "ee-keeya--keeya", while *D. accipitrinus* regularly intersperses its call with a short "tak", e. g., "heeya-heeya, tak-heeya".

> It was seen and heard on a number of occasions, typically in a group of two or more birds. Sometimes perched 20 or more feet apart, they engaged in a sort of conversation in a variety of whistles and sounds, sometimes resembling the squeaks of a rusty gate... Many of the notes uttered in these performances were very similar in both species, call notes and/or visual checks being commonly needed to separate them. (McLoughlin, 1983)

Caiques use a form of behaviour that is known as "crowing". A caique lifts its wings so that they are held momentarily above the head; this reveals the lengthened feathers of the flanks. George Smith (1971) commented:

> When the wings reach the summit the caique gives a "piping toot" which can be a single or a double "pipe". The wings are

then closed. Crowing seems to be a contact or "whereabouts" call. For all caiques within earshot tend to reply with similar crowings. Two birds of a pair may alternately crow, or even crow together. The noise is repeated at several minute intervals. A "low intensity" version also exists, in which the wings are not raised from the body, or just "token" lifted and dropped – rather like a shrugging of the shoulders.

Caiques are among the few parrots that duet. A mated pair will vocalise in a way that sounds like a single bird making a double call note. One bird gives one note and the other replies a second later with a different one, and the same notes are repeated. McLoughlin witnessed dueting, although he did not call it such, but described it perfectly. These performances lasted from a few minutes to, on one occasion, up to half an hour before he left the scene.

Use of the feet

Caiques are highly dexterous, using their feet with great skill to hold or manipulate items. In this respect, and in the dexterity and strength of the feet, they resemble cockatoos. Caiques have the ability to hold the foot further away from the body and higher up than most other parrots when grasping food in the foot while consuming it.

Names

Early authors referred to the Black-headed Caique, the first form described, as the White-breasted Parrot, and even today ornithological literature does not use the word caique. The Yellow--thighed Caique was referred to in the 19th century as the Yellow--throated Parrot.

It can be useful to know the names of caiques in other languages:

	melanocephala	*leucogaster*	*xanthomeria*
German	Grünzügelpapagei	Rostkappenpapagei	Gelbschenkel-Rostkappenpapagei
French	Caique maipourri	Caique a ventre blanc	
Dutch	Zwartcopcaique	Witbuikcaique	
Portuguese	Periquito de cabeça preta	Marianinha	Marianinha de cabeça preta
Spanish	Perico calzoncito		

Spanish names in countries of origin (Rodriguez-Mahecha and Hernandez-Camacho, 2002):

Colombia	Ecuador	Peru	Venezuela
Loro cacique	Chiriclesa	Chirricle cabeza negra	Perico calzoncito
Perico calzoncito	Chirlicles		
Loro guahibo	Loro cabecinegro		
Patilico	Loro coroninegro		

Chapter 2

Captive History

The first record of a caique in captivity outside its native country dates back to 1751. In London a bird dealer in White Hart Yard, near the Strand, acquired one that had been brought from "the Carraccos, on the Continent of America, a part of the Spanish Dominions". Presumably it came from Caracas in Venezuela. George Edwards, Library Keeper at the Royal College of Physicians and author of *Natural History of Birds*, encountered this unknown species. He published a coloured drawing of it, called it the White-breasted Parrot and wrote:

> "I have examined all the Accounts I can find relating to Parrots in different Authors, but can find none that agree with the above-described. It is a very beautiful little Parrot..."

In 1758, Linnaeus, the inventor of the system for classifying animals and plants, named the Black-headed Caique *Psittacus melanocephalus*. At that time he placed all parrots in the genus *Psittacus*. A century later some writers were using the generic name Caica. In 1890 Heine classified the caiques in the genus *Pionites*, which name has been maintained.

The French ornithologist, Count Buffon, wrote about this species in 1779 in his *Histoire Naturelle des Oiseaux*, volume vi, and, in the next volume, published in 1783 included a painting of "La petite Perruche Maypouri, de Cayenne".

As Buffon explained, the name *Maypouri* is that of the tapir, a forest-dwelling hoofed mammal which makes a whistling sound, like the call of a caique. In *Birds in Brazil* Helmut Sick also mentioned the tapir under the White-bellied Caique. He wrote of the latter's voice: "...a strident, prolonged tremulous *tsrrrri-tsrrrri*, in timbre sometimes reminiscent of a tapir call hence the name *'Periquito-d'anta'*, Tapir Parakeet".

Buffon was writing more than 200 years ago – not with total accuracy, yet he knew something about Caiques in the wild. He stated that they did not go near human habitation but kept to flooded forest and flooded savannahs. They made no other sound but the shrill whistle, often repeated in flight, and they never learned to talk. According to Buffon, they flew in small flocks, but often "...without attachment for each other, for they fight frequently and unmercifully: **when some are caught while hunting, there is no means of keeping them alive; they stubbornly refuse to take food and rather starve to death**". Furthermore, he wrote that they were so intractable they could not even be "made docile by blowing tobacco smoke, which is the usual way of training even the most obstinate parrots".

London Zoo purchased a Black-headed Caique in 1855 and two more in 1866 but the species remained largely unknown to Europeans for several decades. Indian people had probably been familiar with its delightful ways for centuries. In 1915 the Rev. C. Dawson was a missionary journeying on the Barama River of Guyana (then British Guyana). He encountered a Black-headed Caique at the farm of a half-cast aboriginal Indian that was:

"...treated like a member of the family, and was as playful as a kitten and as knowing and mischievous as a monkey. The children and he would run races or play hide and seek; and when it was his turn to hide and they couldn't find him, he would come slyly out of his hiding-place and nip the bare foot of the nearest child" (Dawson, 1915).

It was not until about the second decade of the 20th century that a few specimens found their way into the larger collections owned by some of the wealthy aviculturists of the time. One of these, Lady Poltimore, achieved the first recorded breeding of Caiques

in Europe in 1936, from a male Black-headed and a female White-
-bellied. Caiques were also available in the USA, where Gilbert
Lee of California reared the White-bellied in 1932. In 1934 San
Diego Zoo also bred this species. The first consistently successful
breeder was Mrs Williams of Princeton, Florida. Between 1957 and
1964 she reared 34 Black-headed Caiques, including second-gene-
ration young.

The White-bellied Caique was first described in 1820 by
Heinrich Kuhl, a highly respected German ornithologist. He wrote
the first ever monograph of the parrots, *Conspectus Psittacorum*,
despite dying at the early age of 25. The species was still almost
unknown in 1877 when London Zoo received two birds of the
sub-species *xanthomeria* from Iquitos in the Peruvian Amazon. The
Austrian ornithologist, traveller and explorer, Johann Natterer,
who died in 1843, had collected (on the Rio Madeira) the first and
only other live specimen known to science.

The nominate race of the White-bellied Caique (the one with
green thighs), found only in Brazil was described, in 1955, as being
"the most commonly imported species" (in Britain) (Prestwich,
1955). This was before the era of mass importation when most of
the birds imported from Brazil were brought back by seamen.
Many were probably sold to the nearest pet shop to the port of
embarkation. London Zoo acquired its first specimen in 1880.

But caiques were still little known. Greene, in his three-volume
Parrots in Captivity, published in or about 1887, makes no mention
of them, neither does the *Royal Natural History* in its quite extensive parrot section. I believe it was not until the 1960s that they were
imported a little more often. In *Parrots and Related Birds*, published
in the USA in 1959, Henry Bates and Robert Busenbark wrote:

"Rare in this country, the Caiques usually command a premium
price. If the price is based on acclimation efforts, we can assure
the prospective buyer than almost any price would not be too
exorbitant."

Many newly imported caiques refused to take seed; they wanted soft foods, such as banana, and corn on the cob or boiled maize. A newly imported Pallid Caique in my possession in the late 1960s would drink large quantities of nectar made for lories with honey, condensed milk and Benger's Food, also trifle sponge mashed in honey water. They were the only foods for which my caiques then showed real enthusiasm, with the notable exception of walnuts. One had to offer many different kinds of food in the hope of finding something they really liked, in the period before they started to eat seed.

The 1970s was a time of large importations into Europe and the USA of countless parrot species. **Black-headed Caiques** became more freely available. For example, during the period October 1979 to June 1980, 425 Black-headed Caiques were imported into the USA from the country of origin, and only eight White-bellied Caiques. Regular (but not large) consignments have reached Britain since the 1970s. Most of these birds come from Guyana and Suriname, the only countries where caiques are found that still permit the export of parrots.

The following figures show the scale of the export trade in recent years:

	Export quotas		or	Numbers exported	
Exporting country	1997	1998	1999	2000	2001
Guyana	600	600	600	553	494
Suriname	1605	1378	1378	600	477

To put these figures in context, Guyana exported 781 Blue and Yellow Macaws and 6,844 Orange-winged Amazons in the year 2000. As its quota system is probably based more on availability than any other factor, it indicates that Black-headed Caiques are not so easy to obtain. They are not found in large flocks, like Orange-winged Amazons, for example.

The **White-bellied Caique** has always been much rarer in aviculture because the major part of its range is within Brazil, which country has not permitted the export of birds since 1967. These caiques have been exported from Peru and Bolivia. Most of those in captivity probably originate from birds captured in Bolivia.

It is regrettable that any caiques are exported, in this era when breeders can supply the pet and avicultural trade. **The wild-caught birds, being offered at a lower price than captive-bred ones, are bought mainly by ignorant people, unaware of the cruelty that the trade involves, and the high mortality rate after export.** Many of these birds pose a serious disease risk, to other parrots and even to humans.

In the UK George Smith of Peterborough has been the most consistent breeder of caiques over a sustained period. In 1983 he was the first to breed *xanthomeria* and in the following year he bred the nominate race of the White-bellied Caique. In 1991 he wrote:

"Once it becomes generally known what a pure delight a perfectly tame caique can be, extra incentive must be given to breeding the bird to satisfy the pet trade. For as a house pet, the caique can have few equals among parrots."

A decade later caiques had achieved the popularity that these small parrots with huge personalities so richly deserve.

Chapter 3

Care and housing

Caiques are very destructive little parrots. It is as well to bear this in mind when planning an aviary or buying a cage. They could do much damage to unprotected woodwork. An aviary is best constructed from aluminium angle. If the framework is made from wood it will soon appear unsightly and might need to be replaced before long. However, on no account should they be deprived of wood for gnawing. Fresh-cut branches from apple trees are ideal; willow branches will be greatly enjoyed but this softer wood is quickly destroyed.

The provision of sufficient wood for gnawing is something that should be carefully considered before a caique is purchased. It is an important factor in keeping one of these little parrots happy and healthy. A young hand-reared Black-headed Caique that I observed periodically in a local pet shop had a very overgrown beak by the time it was nine months old. It had never been provided with wood to gnaw.

Lack of a rough surface (such as natural bark) for the feet to grip can result in overgrown nails, even before a caique is one year old. This problem is not difficult to cure. Cutting the nails is not recommended as this can stimulate growth. The answer is to obtain a sand-covered perch (available from specialist parrot suppliers) as the slightly rough surface wears down the nails. These perches are moulded to different shapes and provide exercise for the feet. Such perches are recommended for caiques, rather than concrete ones.

Wood is beneficial not only to keep the beak in good condition but also to allow a caique to reveal an interesting aspect of its behaviour. As I recorded in *The Parrots of South America*:

"An area of the branch is immediately stripped of bark and the body is rubbed, cat-like against it, first on one side, then on the other. So absorbed does the bird become in these vigorous, almost frantic movements that I am invariably reminded of a bird anting. These movements are carried out equally enthusiastically on a twig completely stripped of bark, or on a dry but bark-covered one. If I held a twig vertically, my Pallid Caique would rub himself against it for minutes at a time, and would even sharpen the end to a point to obtain a more satisfying effect."

For a pet caique a big effort should be made to renew the wooden perches in the cage on a regular basis. Perches of a synthetic material, such as plastic, are totally unsuitable. It is advisable to have a supply of wooden perches cut to size, ready to replace one that has been gnawed through.

Indoor cage

A pet caique needs a larger cage than its size suggests because it will be very active and inventive. Playing with toys and rolling around on its back (perhaps juggling a nut in its feet) are activities that would be difficult to carry out in a confined space. A twiggy branch also takes up space. My recommendation is to buy a cage substantially larger than those sold for Cockatiels. Remove the grid. Caiques love to play on the floor, rolling around or hiding in newspaper. This would be difficult if the grid was in place. It can be inserted while the tray is cleaned if the caique has to stay inside his cage at this time.

The cage should have at least some sides with horizontal bars, for ease of climbing. It should be longer than it is high as this design offers more opportunity for exercise and play. Cylindrical cages should be avoided – in fact they should be banned as unsuitable for all birds.

Toys are extremely important for caiques as these parrots are naturally so active and playful. Position them carefully for maximum enjoyment. For example, a rope ladder with a bell hanging within reach will give hours of enjoyment. Rotate toys on a regular basis and clean them when they are not in use. Examine them for safety and try to visualise potential dangers. Look at ropes and other toys as potentially lethal (sadly parrots have been strangled by them) if not properly presented.

In addition to toys and branches, the cage can contain a cloth pouch or "bed" made especially for small parrots such as caiques and conures. Most caiques love to snuggle down into one at night while others will burrow under the newspaper on the floor of the cage. They have an unusual habit of pulling toys to the entrance of their sleeping place, to block the opening.

In my opinion, newspaper is a good material with which to cover the cage floor. It is entirely safe (newsprint does not contain lead these days) and easily obtainable. It is also quick to change; several layers of paper can line the cage floor and several sheets can be removed twice a day. After a bath, all the paper must be removed. The only disadvantage from the perspective of the caique owner is that the white breast of his bird might become a little smutty from the newsprint! Another floor option that might be considered is wood chips made for animal beds. Sand and sawdust are not recommended as they are too fine and make such a mess. Whatever the floor covering, it should be changed daily (or in the case of wood chips, the area under the perch) to prevent uneaten fruit from becoming mouldy.

Take a careful look at the door catch on your caique's cage. These little parrots are strong enough and clever enough to undo some cage doors. Think ahead and put a dog clip or a padlock on the cage.

Keeping the walls clean

Caiques are messy feeders, flicking pieces of fruit in all directions. In the house or birdroom or in the indoor part of an outdoor aviary, it is advisable to prepare the walls for ease of cleaning. In the house the walls around the cage can be covered with a washable surface such as Fablon, a self-adhesive material available in many colours and patterns. Elsewhere the walls can be covered in clear plastic that is easy to wipe down.

Position of cage

Caiques, like other parrots, are highly social and inquisitive. They want to be where the action is! Excluding the kitchen, the most lived-in room in the house is where your caique will want to be. The kitchen is not recommended because of the often rapidly--changing temperature and humidity, as a result of cooking, and because of the lethal fumes associated with Teflon-coated kitchen utensils. The hazards while cooking is in progress are obvious.

The cage is best placed in an alcove, or in a position where it is protected by a wall on two sides. It should not be possible to walk right round the cages as a parrot in such a location is vulnerable to many forms of stress, especially from visitors who are unaware of how easily a parrot can be frightened by unfamiliar objects. A location that is protected on two sides provides a sense of security. Although caiques are not usually nervous birds and most of those available are captive-bed, this principle still holds good.

Parrots love to be able to see out of the window but the cage should not be in direct sunlight unless blinds can be used when sunlight would reach the cage. Also remember that a small parrot in a cage presents a tempting sight to less honest passers by. Don't display your bird as though he is in a shop window! Your caique's cage does not need to be covered at night unless it is in a position where car headlights or street lights could shine into the room.

Should your caique be kept near a radiator? If there is a choice of location the answer is "no". Birds from dry habitats, such as Cockatiels, can tolerate a dry environment. Caiques come from rainforest areas where the humidity is high. A dry environment is unnatural. While most rooms are centrally heated, some parts of the room will be dryer than others so avoid these areas when positioning the cage. A recently weaned hand-reared young bird might require a slightly higher temperature than normal room temperature but other caiques do not need additional heat.

Aviaries and breeding cages

For most parrots it is recommended that aviaries for breeding pairs should be as large as possible. However, this does not apply to caiques, because they are not strong flyers. They breed best in cages or flights about 8ft (2.4m) long. Even tame birds can take off suddenly and hit the wire mesh when frightened.

Caiques do well in outdoor aviaries or suspended cages in warm climates. In cooler climates, such as that of northern Europe, the best quality of life is offered by keeping pairs in flights or cages inside a building with access to outdoor aviaries except in bad weather. It is worth noting that caiques, unlike most parrots, actually like holes and tunnels. Therefore if you wish to build an outside aviary but it cannot be built flat against the building in which they are kept, it could be connected by a tunnel.

Welded mesh

Ready-made panels of welded mesh can be bought for sides and roof, also panels containing a door. These are ready to erect, unless you wish to paint them first. It is advisable to double-wire the aviary. The extra cost and labour will repay you in injuries averted. Caiques can be very aggressive, especially when breeding. I refer not only to the dangers to the birds in the next aviary from bitten feet and even ripped-off upper mandibles, but also to attacks from owls, birds of prey and cats. It is a sad fact that many birds have had a leg ripped off through welded mesh by one of these predators. This is impossible if the aviary is double-wired.

The suggested size of welded mesh to use is 1 in × 1/2 in, or 1/2 in square, of 14g or 12g. Thinner mesh should not be used as caiques are capable of biting through it. A friend told me how her parrots were kept in temporary aviaries when she moved house. One day she heard the sound of birds shrieking in fear. Hurrying to the aviaries she found that a caique had bitten through the welded mesh of its cage and through that of the adjoining cage to enter and attack its neighbours, a pair of lorikeets. They would undoubtedly have been killed if she had not intervened in time. The caiques were going to nest, causing the male to become very aggressive. This demonstrates that parrots can live within unsuitable mesh until something disturbs them, when they can bite their way out with ease.

Secluded aviaries

Unlike Australian parakeets, for example, many of which inhabit open country, and which thrive in open aviaries, caiques prefer more enclosed, secluded aviaries. In the wild they spend most of their time in the tree canopy in forest, usually dense forest. In an outdoor aviary, they feel more at ease in an aviary with solid sides and only one side and part of the roof not covered in. It is seldom easy to provide leafy branches on a regular basis, but ideally caique aviaries should be filled with them! Suitable trees are apple, pear, willow, ash, elm, hazel, hawthorn and poplar, also, in subtropical and tropical countries, casuarinas.

Unfortunately, these branches do not last long because caiques are so destructive – but there is no pastime that keeps them so happily occupied as gnawing fresh branches and rubbing themselves against them. A real effort should be made to provide these branches on a regular basis. They should be thoroughly washed to remove grime and birds' droppings.

Aviary floor

Some thought should be given to the aviary floor, which must be easy to keep clean. Concrete might be used but will need to be scrubbed or pressure washed on occasions. A more practical and attractive alternative is small stones. If you are buying from a builders' merchant ask for 20mm gravel, which costs about £18 a ton. For an aviary 8ft (2.4m) long and 3ft (91cm) wide, you will need a quarter of a ton. You can lay the stones directly on to existing turf or lawn. In time, the grass will grow up through the stones and create an interesting environment for the caiques. The stones are very easy to keep clean with the use of a pressure washer. Another option for the aviary floor is large paving slabs laid on washed sand. This is the quick method if you do not like laying concrete.

Italian aviculturist Paolo Bertagnolio recorded curious behaviour by his caiques. They excavated the gravel floor of their flight, resting their face against the ground then rapidly casting a rain of gravel backwards with alternate movements of the legs. The heap of gravel that accumulated would have filled a wheelbarrow! (Bertagnolio, 1974). One advantage of giving caiques access to an outdoor aviary is that it is possible to observe all kinds of interesting behaviours that are not seen in caged birds.

Enriching the indoor environment

A number of breeders keep caiques in an enclosed building outside their house. The quality of life for birds kept in this way is usually poor. An effort should be made to improve the environment with the use of plants and windows that admit a good amount of natural light. Plants add enormously to the creation of a pleasant environment. Few private aviculturists could create a wonderful house for neotropical parrots such as that at Plantaria bird park, near Kevelaer in Germany, but even a few trailing plants hung from the ceiling will remove the stark atmosphere found in many buildings in which parrots are expected to breed. Parrots also appreciate greenness and beauty!

Pairs in aviaries will also enjoy items to keep them occupied, such as swings, ropes and bells.

Access to water

Caiques are enthusiastic bathers. Those in aviaries should have large shallow receptacles for bathing, preferably in the outdoor part of the aviary, as well as a smaller dish of water to drink near the food. In a hot or dry climate, it is worthwhile fitting a sprinkler over a caique aviary. They enjoy bathing in wet vegetation. Birds kept indoors can be sprayed with water from a plant mister, allowed to bathe in the sink or even taken into the shower. Caiques are the only parrots I know that will rub themselves dry on a towel! Some will even rub themselves over their favourite human's hair! They love water – and they need it to keep their plumage in good condition. Some of them are not satisfied until they are thoroughly drenched. I have heard of caiques being dried after a bath with a hair-drier on a low setting but my own opinion is that hair dryers should be kept away from parrots!

Chapter 4

Diet and Nutrition

Caiques are a pleasure to feed because they are willing to sample such a wide range of items. They love their food! In fact, unlike other parrots, they will guard it in an almost dog-like manner and absolutely refuse to share, even in a closely bonded pair. Whereas an Amazon or a lory, for example, will good-naturedly let its mate take food from its beak, a caique will never permit this.

Caiques are fruit-eaters. They require a lot of soft foods in their diet and I would suggest that fruit forms a minimum of 35% of their intake. Experimentation is necessary as individual caiques vary considerably in their preferences. A wide variety of tropical fruits are available so good use should be made of these, in order to provide as much variety as possible.

Fruits

Acceptable fruits are apples (mainly for the pips), oranges, cherries, sweet grapes, pomegranates, sweet oranges (especially juicy Satsumas) and pears. It is seasonal soft fruits such as redcurrants, blueberries, raspberries, blackberries and cranberries that they really love, the latter three for their tiny pips. It is not a good idea to offer blackberries and elderberries and other fruits that stain heavily to caiques kept indoors! These soft berries (also hawthorn berries) can be frozen for use throughout the year. It does not matter that the flesh of the fruit is somewhat soggy after freezing as they are only interested in the pips (seeds).

Orange should be offered with skin intact in small pieces. It is likely to be ignored unless the orange is sweet. Tropical fruits that caiques enjoy are papaya, guava, kiwi and cactus fruit. To feed the latter just cut it into quarters. It should be fed ripe, not hard. It is mainly the seeds in kiwi, cactus and guava that attract them. They also like mango; this can be offered in small pieces with the skin still adhering.

Pomegranates are among the healthiest fruits available. They are loaded with Vitamin B_2 (riboflavin) and contain manganese, one of the essential trace elements. Caiques and other parrots love the translucent red seeds contained in these fruits. The redness of the skin indicates the ripeness of the fruit. If one is cut open when the interior is whitish, the fruit will be ignored. Pomegranates should be cut into pieces, leaving the skin intact. In northern Europe the season of availability is from September to December. To extend the season, one can buy a number of cases, wrap each fruit individually in newspaper and store them in a cool place.

In the days when only imported birds were available, they had been fed on banana. Banana is an excellent food that contains various trace elements. One fresh banana is said to contain as much as 185mg of potassium, 16mg of magnesium, 13mg of phosphorus, 135mg of chlorine, 60mg of sulphur, 4mg of calcium, traces of iodine and bromine and 95iu of Vitamin A. Few caiques eat more than a couple of slices of banana a day; nevertheless, they might be obtaining elements that are lacking from many other food items. One needs to learn the degree of ripeness that appeals to each individual bird. The banana should be cut across the fruit (in round sections) and offered in the skin in a foot-convenient size. Some caiques do not like fresh banana but many like the crunchy banana chips obtainable from health food stores. These should be limited as they have a high fat content.

Stone fruits such as peaches and plums can be offered but might be refused. Apricots are very healthy, with a high Vitamin A content, if one can persuade caiques to eat them. They also contain essential trace elements – iron, copper and phosphorus – and, in their dried form, contain more protein than any other dried fruit.

It is important to wash most fruits before they are fed, as they might have been sprayed with harmful chemicals. Fruits such as apple should be crisp and grapes and pear should be firm, not overripe. A mixture of soft fruits should be avoided as it ends up as a sludgy mixture that will ferment in hot weather and attract insects. Chose with care the fruits that are placed in the same container. In outdoor aviaries especially it is better to feed two fruits two or three times a day rather than mix them all and offer them at one feed.

Sultanas and raisins are rich in potassium and iron. They are relished after being soaked in water for a few hours, until they are soft and plump. Dried figs are also rich in minerals. They can be offered dry or soaked and contain tiny, crunchy seeds.

Fresh fruits should be offered in a stainless steel container, separate from dry food items. For added enjoyment, whole or half fruits can be hung up on a stainless steel holder (obtainable from pet stores) or spiked on to a perch in the aviary. If a bird refuses to eat certain fruits, they are more likely to be sampled in this manner – disguised as playthings rather than food items. I have even hung fruits from branches to try to tempt them.

Initially a seed mixture containing a good variety of seeds should be offered to observe which ones are eaten. Small seeds, with the exception of hemp, might be ignored. However, sunflower seed should not be fed *ad lib.*

Pellets

This form of food is most useful for species such as the Grey Parrot, many individuals of which cannot be persuaded to eat much fresh food. This is not a problem with caiques in which dietary deficiencies as a result of a limited diet are rare or unknown. My own opinion in that processed food such as pellets and extruded foods are no healthier for parrots than they are for humans, and should be offered to caiques in small quantities, if at all.

Vegetables

Fresh vegetables are not always eaten with the same enthusiasm as fruit. Those offered can include sugar snap peas, young, tender peas in the pod, raw or par-boiled carrot, green beans, chopped courgettes and celery. Red bell peppers and their seeds are enjoyed. Red bell peppers are more beneficial than green or yellow because they contain more beta carotene, the precursor to Vitamin A. Some caiques like the hot chilli peppers. In the USA sweet potatoes and yams are also used. Frozen peas and frozen sweetcorn, thawed, are also relished. Fresh corn, light yellow, soft and tender, is a great favourite. It should be offered in small pieces, raw. Older corn is harder and is more acceptable after being lightly cooked or frozen.

Mash/rearing food

For caiques that are less adventurous in their choice of food, also for those rearing young, it is worth making a mash of various items. Ingredients can include a pack of mixed frozen vegetables (carrots, peas, sweetcorn) and a few soaked or cooked pulses added to hard-boiled egg, carrot and wholegrain bread that have been blended in a food mixer. Chopped walnuts sprinkled on top will encourage the caiques to sample this food. It provides the protein essential for pairs rearing young and a much wider range of nutrients than those found in any seed mixture. It is an ideal softfood, easily digested, for young caiques at the weaning stage. There are some parrot rearing foods on the market that contain egg – but the quality varies.

Nuts

Caiques adore walnuts. Halves with or without the shell can be given in moderation – perhaps two halves per bird per day. Although caiques like peanuts they carry the risk of aflatoxins (a toxic compound produced by a mould fungus). If peanuts are fed, this should be in moderation and with human-grade nuts bought in a health food store – but as walnuts are even more acceptable, it is not worth taking the risk. Salted nuts and other salted food must be avoided. Almonds in the shell will amuse caiques for hours before they finally penetrate the shell.

Livefood

Some caiques relish mealworms and other livefood. As an additional source of protein (admittedly an expensive one), mealworms and waxmoth larvae are suitable for pairs rearing young.

Grit and cuttlefish bone

Grit is swallowed by seed-eating birds to grind food in the gizzard. Grit can be offered to caiques but as their diet contains a large proportion of soft items, it is perhaps not necessary for this purpose. Mineral grit contains valuable minerals that could be missing from the diet. It will not be necessary if a mineral supplement made for parrots is offered on occasions. Cuttlefish bone is not necessary for pet birds but will be consumed by females prior to egg-laying. In theory, the calcium in cuttlefish bone cannot be absorbed by birds unless they have access to sunlight or a diet containing Vitamin D3.

When feeding caiques, the emphasis should be on a varied diet of fresh, quality foods.

1. Black-headed Caique *(P. m. melanocephala)*

2. Black-headed Caique aged about seven weeks

3. Fearless and inquisitive, a Black-headed Caique investigates a parrot robot

4. Wing-lifting behaviour accompanied by excited calls – known as "crowing"

5. Black-headed Caique swaying in typical caique manner

6. L-shaped nest-box as seen from the back, showing the inspection door

7. Young pair of White-bellied Caiques *(P. l. leucogaster)* in Brazil

8.–9. *P. l. leucogaster* (left) and *P. l. xanthomeria* (right) enjoying fresh-cut branches

10. Yellow-thighed Caique *P. L. xanthomeria* demonstrate the typically playful behaviour of Caiques

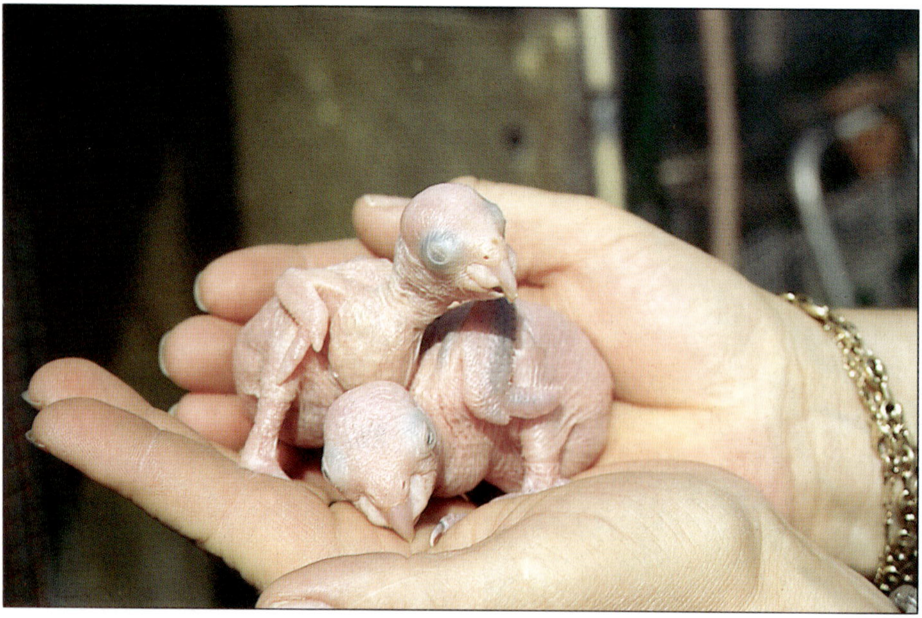

11. *P. l. xanthomeria* a few days old; note the raised pads on the upper mandible

Chapter 5

Caiques as Pets

In 1779 Count Buffon wrote of caiques caught in the wild: "If they are to be reared they must be caught young, and they would not be worth the trouble of rearing, if their plumage were not so beautiful and their form so remarkable."

He stated that they were so stubborn they would starve to death rather than eat. Writing in 1887, Sclater did not agree. "The *Caica (melanocephala)* is remarkable for its excessive friendliness and sociability. I brought a specimen of it home with me (from British Guyana), which is certainly the tamest bird I have ever come across."

Buffon's were probably the first words written on the suitability of caiques as pets. Today this is not in doubt. These jaunty little parrots are universally acclaimed. Probably no one knows caiques better than George Smith, a retired vet, who has been breeding them since 1972 – just over 30 years. He summed up their attributes as follows:

Caiques make nearly perfect pocket-edition pet parrots. Their smallish size, preference for walking and climbing rather than flying, haughty arrogance, fearlessness, extroverted personalities, curious and boisterous natures, and their pretty colours make them quite enchanting. Caiques make good companion pets because they like attention and, when in the mood, even want to be cuddled. They can be taught to talk and may become whispering chatterboxes (Smith, 1996).

An American breeder, Nancy Weaver, described them as having:

"...more energy than the EverReady bunny. Well-adjusted, tame caiques are seemingly programmed by nature to make a game out of life itself... Tame caiques have charming personalities. In addition to being mischievous and inquisitive, hand-reared caiques are fearless and headstrong, and can find trouble easily" (Weaver, 1995).

Another American breeder, Barbara Hine, aptly commented:

"No species could exhibit more exuberance and love of life than the caique. Whatever they're doing, it's full-speed-ahead, non-stop activity, and they are totally engrossed in their endeavors" (Hine, 1997).

If you want a parrot that can talk well, that needs a minimum amount of time devoted to preparing its food, that is always predictable and sweet-natured, a caique is not for you. But if you want a bundle of fun and energy that will mesmerise you with its antics, make compulsive viewing and brighten your day, consider a caique! But you must be prepared for its shrill voice, wilful personality and its powers of destruction. If you can tolerate these minor "defects", you will have found a fascinating companion with whom to share your life.

One major advantage of the outgoing personality of caiques is that they do not become stressed easily, tolerating situations that would cause a Grey Parrot, for example, to start to pluck itself. Plucking in caiques due to stress must be very rare (if it exists). I have never seen or heard of a plucked one except in the case of breeding birds that might remove feathers from the thighs or breast to line the nest.

Purchasing a hand-reared youngster

My advice to someone seeking a young bird is to go directly to the breeder. The best age to buy is soon after it is weaned, that is, at about 14 weeks – possibly a little older. In Europe nearly all breeders wean their young and sell them when they are capable of feeding themselves. In the USA few breeders wean their young. Most are sold to pet stores or even to those wanting a pet before they are weaned. This is a bad practice that often ends in the death of the parrot a short while later. The problem in purchasing (weaned or unweaned) from pet stores where there are other parrots, Cockatiels or Budgerigars, is that young parrots are very susceptible to contracting disease because their immune systems are not fully functional. When birds from different sources are brought together, diseases proliferate. The other problem, where pet stores buy unweaned young, is that they are not always capable of weaning them correctly, so the purchaser inherits a problem bird from the start.

The other reason to buy direct from the breeder is that wild--caught Black-headed Caiques are still being imported into Europe from Guyana and Suriname. People with little knowledge of parrots will be unable to distinguish a wild-caught caique from a captive-bred one. Wild-caught birds are likely to be nervous or unfriendly (unless young), they are often in poor feather, usually in poor health (although they might appear healthy) and they are not wearing a *closed* ring (band).

All reputable breeders put closed rings on their young ones. Imported birds might be wearing a ring, perhaps a narrow stainless steel one, but it is of the type that can be fitted to a bird at any age. A breeder's ring usually is marked with his or her initials, the year of hatch (sometimes marked sideways to the other letters and numbers) and a serial number that identifies the individual bird.

Fortunately, it is easy to distinguish a young caique from an adult (see Chapter 1) so the informed purchaser should not make a mistake if he or she decides not to buy from a breeder. Whatever the source, the bird should be alert, in good feather and friendly. It does not matter if the whitish breast feathers are slightly dirty;

young caiques are so playful that, especially if kept in a cage with newspaper, their underparts will not look clean.

The purchaser of a young bird should ask for its hatch date. A good breeder will usually provide a hatch certificate so, before purchase, check the hatch date to ensure that the caique is not younger than 13 weeks. The purchaser should also ask for a sample of the food on which it has been reared, and of other foods that it has been eating. This is because on being moved to a new home young parrots often suffer from weaning regression. That is, they do not eat very well for a few days. This does not matter if the seller has shown the purchaser how the young bird has been hand-fed and provided some food. Hand-feeding should, in my opinion, be continued once or twice daily, during the transition period. If the young caique is eating well and does not want to be hand-fed, it can be discontinued. If it is eating well but still enjoys being hand-fed, continue once daily for as long as it wants it. This might be for several months! However, the owner who can hand-feed a caique has a huge advantage if it is necessary to give medication, vitamins or calcium, as this can easily be added to the food. If the caique has been syringe-fed and the new owner is nervous of doing this, he or she should use a teaspoon (warmed slightly) with the sides bent inwards a little. The food must, of course, be given warm – but not boiling hot.

A major reason for the death of recently weaned parrots is that the new owner is told that they are weaned and immediately offers a diet that consists mainly of seed or of pellets. Immature parrots need soft foods that are easy to digest. Young caiques should be offered lots of fruit, perhaps a mash (as described in Chapter 4) and any other soft items that are suitable such as wholegrain bread, warm cooked peas and sweetcorn, tender pieces of corn on the cob and cooked pasta. Emphasis should be on the soft foods although the harder items can be available. As long as a young bird can make the choice it will not suffer weight loss or listlessness during the transition period.

Young caiques are quite simply adorable, so sweet and playful – most of the time! However, they can be extremely dominant towards other parrots, even much larger ones. The breeder needs to be aware that two or three caiques could "gang up" on other young parrots being hand-fed and badly frighten them or even injure them.

Parent-reared and wild-caught caiques

Occasionally captive-bred parent-reared caiques are offered for sale. If they are young, they are just as suitable for pets as hand-reared birds. It will probably take only a short time to tame them, as caiques are more amenable to taming than most parrots. It also helps to use favoured food items as "bribes"! An adult bird is a different matter. Many factors are involved and whether or not it would make a good pet is impossible to predict.

For ethical reasons, I would not recommend the purchase of a wild-caught caique. Bear in mind for every one that reaches Europe, a number will have died including, perhaps, chicks in the nest, left to starve, adults that cannot adjust to a captive diet and caiques of all ages that have died as a result of contracting disease in insanitary (often filthy) holding stations.

Handling

Caiques are in the top league of parrots, along with the white cockatoos, that love to be handled if they are tame. As well as enjoying being held or having their heads scratched, unlike most parrots, they like contact all over the body. Snuggling up to a human friend or even snuggling under his or her clothes is a favourite pastime. They are also happy to lie in the hand on their back, something that the tamest of other parrots will not usually tolerate for more than a few seconds.

Time out of the cage

Caiques have a bigger potential for finding trouble than almost any other parrot. This is due to a combination of intense curiosity and total fearlessness. For this reason a caique must *never* be left unattended outside its cage. This is to protect its own safety and because it could be extremely destructive, damaging furniture, books, curtains and other items that are expensive to replace. All the obvious hazards such as house plants, items containing lead and zinc, biros, pencils and jewellery, must be beyond its reach.

I am normally strongly against the habit of wing-clipping pet parrots because it so greatly reduces their quality of life and their health over the long term. However, in the case of caiques, who run, hop and climb perhaps even more than they fly, and are extremely active birds, I doubt that wing-clipping reduces their enjoyment of life. Indeed, it is hard to curb the *joie de vivre* of a tame caique. Wing-clipping limits to only a small degree the areas to which it has access, although being such a skilful climber, a caique can reach places that other parrots would not think of going – especially holes and small openings. For this reason any room in which a caique is to have its freedom should be carefully examined. Is there a space behind the back of the fire? Is there a crevice behind an item of furniture? Are there exposed electric leads or cables that a caique might bite into with fatal consequences? All these possibilities must be considered very carefully – because if a caique *can* find trouble, it *will* do so. Every effort must be made to prevent accidents. There is nothing so sad as to lose a beloved parrot due to carelessness or failure to visualise potentially disastrous situations.

Play stands

A caique needs an area away from its cage that is the focus of its attention when it is let out. This area should be provided from the outset, before it acquires bad habits, such as gnawing doors or pelmets. Parrots should, in any case, be discouraged from landing in such places. The play stand should be provided with ropes, swings, perhaps a roll of kitchen towel, apple or willow twigs, and anything else that will keep a caique amused, such as a carrot with the green top intact. Caiques tend to have short attention spans so keep an eye on them and, if necessary, rotate toys and items of destruction.

How do you return a strong-willed little caique to its cage if it does not want to go? Pit your wits, not your force, against it! Do not chase it about. Place a tempting item of food inside its cage, pretend not to watch it and shut the door quickly when it returns. If all else fails, throw a towel over it.

Biting

As it matures, the personality of a caique (especially a male) can change dramatically – and the owner must be prepared for this. The fact is that caiques can bite very hard and apparently without provocation. Whereas anyone who knows a Grey or an Amazon parrot can read their behaviour and easily see when trouble is brewing, caiques are so fast in everything they do and mercurial in their emotions, that they can attack suddenly and without warning. They can bite extremely hard and hang on relentlessly.

No parrot is perfect in a pet situation – and the tendency to bite is the disadvantage of some caiques. While it is impossible to change their personalities, making rules from the outset and sticking to them will minimise problems of dominance and aggression.

Right from the start adopt these rules:

➡ Do not allow your caique to sit on your shoulder. In this position your eyes, ears, face and nose are vulnerable. This is especially the case if your bird is sitting there when you are approached by someone it does not like or, in fact, anyone else if this causes jealousy. Unable to attack the other person, it will bite you instead. Your caique can perch on your hand or lay in your lap.

➼ Teach you caique to step on to your hand. Using the words "Step up!" will help to reinforce this. In a young bird it is very simple to teach this simply by slowly moving your hand towards it and pressing your index finger against its breast, just above its feet. Practice this daily. You must be able to pick up your caique when you need to return it to its cage – perhaps in an emergency.

Also, this simple command is the first step towards your caique's realisation that you are in control. Caiques have *extremely* strong, wilful personalities and if you allow them to do what they want from the outset, your relationship with your caique will not progress smoothly. Your soft cuddly baby could turn into a feathered demon if it does not know what kind discipline is.

➼ Do not allow it to spend hours and hours out of the cage. If you do, it will treat the house as though it is its territory and will attack people who enter who it does not like. It is a wise precaution to confine an adult caique to its cage when an unknown person enters the house. Assess its reaction to this person before letting it out. If possible, introduce the two in a room away from the caique's cage (the area where it is most territorial).

➼ If your caique has a box to retire to at night, be aware that giving it a small ball or anything that resembles an egg that it takes into the box, could result in very aggressive behaviour. It could defend this item and the box as though it was breeding.

If you intend to breed with your caique in the future, do not offer play items that resemble eggs; the foundation of a bad habit (egg-breaking) could result.

If I have over-emphasised the sometimes aggressive nature of caiques it is because I want to make owners aware of problems that can arise and to encourage them to act in a way which makes these problems less likely to materialise. One owner wrote of her caique:

> "If she is tired, she will bite. If she is over-stimulated, she will bite. It is her way; it is my responsibility to protect her from being over-stimulated and to protect other people and animals from her. I cannot blame her for my failure to control the situation" (Tyson, 2003).

This caring caique owner had the right attitude! When a caique bites, try to work out why and avoid a similar situation in future. It might be because it does not want to be handled at that moment; perhaps it wants to sleep or to eat. Respect its wishes! Another circumstance in which pet caiques bite is when they are in breeding condition. The flashing eyes and swaggering gait should alert the owner to this state; it could last for a couple of months. During this time the bird should be carefully observed. Learn to read its body language!

A caique might also bite out of fear. This is unlikely to apply to a hand-reared bird unless a sudden loud sound or careless action on someone's part frightened it badly.

One caique, or two?

Introducing a second caique to the household when the first is well established can be difficult or downright dangerous. About one year after Darlene Friedman bought her Black-headed Caique she decided to obtain a young female White-bellied. This is what happened:

My sweet, friendly Kiwi turned into a vicious attempted murderer the second he saw Rainbow for the first time. I couldn't believe that a bird who had coexisted so peacefully with my two other parrots would be capable of showing such frenzied rage. Had I not separated them, I'm sure he would have torn her limb from limb (Friedman, 2001).

There is an important lesson to be learned here. It is a big mistake to introduce a caique into what an established caique considers to be its territory. Whether it is a cage, aviary or room, the result is the same. The introduction must occur on neutral ground. When Darlene Friedman realised that this was the correct procedure, Kiwi gradually started to tolerate Rainbow's presence.

Several times he went over to her and either bit her or bumped her so she'd fall over onto her back. After about one week of this, I was watching them on the floor when he ran over to her and once again knocked her flat on her back. She jumped right back up and knocked him onto his back! He lay there, feet up in the air, with an astonished look on his face. Then he slowly puffed out the feathers on his face, and uttered a sound that he only makes when he's having great fun That was the turning point.

A few weeks later the two caiques played together all day and slept together at night. But the outcome could have been very different – a fatal conclusion, in fact – if the importance of neutral territory had been ignored.

Caiques can be either very affectionate or very spiteful towards other birds in the household. Because they are fearless, they do not hesitate to attack parrots much larger than themselves. On the other hand, they can befriend a bird as a large as a cockatoo or a macaw, snuggling up to it and sleeping under its wing! Caiques can also terrorise other household pets, including cats and dogs, and take a malicious enjoyment in doing so. It is most unfair to allow this, especially as a parrot's bite can be serious. There is never a dull moment with little white-breasted parrots!

Mimicry

Caiques readily learn to whistle because such a sound is close to their natural calls. As long ago as the 1870s Stolzmann remarked on this talent. He wrote that caiques learn to whistle perfectly but are not capable of grasping any melody (unlike Amazon parrots, for example). The scale of their voice is fairly extensive and their whistling is pure. As soon as they begin to whistle they seize the notes, but interpret the melody in their own way. They conclude without any discord the melodies started for them, but always in their own style. One caique known to Stolzmann would whistle in all positions, perched, lying on its back, or hanging head down from a branch, always with the same purity and intensity.

Caiques are not able to mimic the human voice very realistically and use what one owner described as a cartoon character voice. They can learn a few words, however. One owner of a White-bellied stated that the bird's enunciation was poor and she often failed to complete the phrases, but her tone was musical. Her first words were "Pretty, pretty bird" and "Tep up".

Shrieking

If caiques are persistently noisy it might be because their contact call goes unanswered. Caiques, like all parrots, call to each other to keep in contact. If that call is answered they are reassured that their mate (human or otherwise) is close by. If they are ignored, they will continue to call. If the shrieking continues, it is a mistake to shout at the bird to be quiet. The trick is to persuade him to change the shrieking into another sound. With some

Amazon parrots who love to sing, it is easy to stop them yelling by singing, then they will join in. Caiques cannot sing but they love to whistle, so whistle and they will join in! It is a good idea to teach a caique to whistle a tune or two for this reason, as well as for their entertainment and your enjoyment.

Pay careful attention to the psychological and physical welfare of your caique and you could have this wonderful companion for two or three decades.

Chapter 6

Breeding Caiques

Caiques have one enormous advantage over most parrots from the perspective of the breeder. They do not need large aviaries, and some breeders think that they do better in cages. This is partly because they appreciate a secluded environment, and partly because as they are not strong flyers they probably feel more secure. A suitable size for a pair is about 8ft (2.4m) long, 20in (50cm) wide and 20in high. Small aviaries and indoor flights can also be used. In colder climates, the aviary should have a fully enclosed shelter or an inside area inside a birdroom. In Germany, for example, a successful breeder of the Black-headed Caique kept his pair in an aviary with an outside flight 10ft (3m) long × 3ft 4in (1m) wide and 6ft 8in (2m) high with an inside aviary 8ft 4in (2.5m) long, 32in (80cm) wide and 6ft 8in (2m) high (Brockner, 1992). This is larger than would be provided by most breeders. Also, the inside part does not need to be full-depth (walk-in) and is easier to keep clean (and less invasive when cleaning occurs) if it is raised about 3ft (91cm) above the floor.

Although caiques have been kept in a colony, in such circumstances it is likely that only the dominant pair will breed. At Busch Gardens, Tampa, Florida, the family colony of White--bellied Caiques on exhibit there for many years produced nume-rous young. When I saw then in the 1980s all the birds used the same large box for roosting and breeding. At one time four females were raising seven young between them! This success might have been due to the fact that they were a close-knit family. In contrast, at Paradise Park in Cornwall, in the UK, four pairs of White-bellied

Caiques were kept together for about five years without breeding. When they were separated, one pair per aviary, two pairs were rearing chicks by the following April (at the time of going to press).

Caiques probably breed best when there are other pairs in fairly close proximity but not so close as to be an intrusion into a pair's territory. This might cause stress. However, one of the first really successful breeders of Black-headed Caiques was Tom Ireland in Florida. His pairs were housed in a row of all-wire cages supported on a frame about 3ft (91cm) off the ground, with only about 2in (5cm) between each cage! The first female would lay at the end of December and within a couple of weeks most of the other ten or so pairs would also be on eggs. The diet of his birds included large quantities of fresh corn on the cob, other vegetables and fruits and a mixture of wholemeal bread, grated carrot and endive.

One disadvantage of keeping caiques in cages is that their beaks and claws are likely to become overgrown unless an enormous effort is made to provide fresh-cut branches at frequent intervals. Even so, the claws might need to be trimmed unless stout branches are available. If the claws are long and curved they are a hazard and can prevent a caique from moving around easily on the wire mesh of the cage.

Obtaining a pair

As in many parrots, there are more males than females in captivity. Unscrupulous people will sell two males as a pair to anyone unwise enough to buy adult birds. The disadvantages of buying adults include unknown age and history and, often, lack of proof of sex. As caiques can breed when between two and three years old, there is not a long wait for young birds to mature. Anyone who does not have the patience to wait a couple of years is unlikely to have the right temperament to breed parrots.

Patience is essential! The advantages of buying young birds are: known age, and untried (not rejected) breeding birds. In addition, they will adapt more readily to new and different management.

Sexing

Male and female are alike in appearance. Colour and beak size are not significant, so DNA sexing is recommended. This can be carried out from the age of seven weeks onwards. Surgical sexing is not recommended. Some vets have found that caiques are inclined to react adversely to anaesthetic, so this should be avoided unless absolutely essential. Surgical sexing is not essential – and is often inaccurate.

Some relative differences in behaviour and appearance between males and females have been suggested, but they are not accurate. Behaviour can be totally misleading. Two males might feed each other and copulate and two females might appear just as closely bonded as a male and a female. During copulation, a female might mount a male, which could be very confusing to the observer. A female might briefly feed a male.

Before the days of surgical sexing inaccurate ideas abounded regarding sex determination in parrots. Writing in 1935 about his Black-headed Caiques, A. C. Furner recorded that on many occasions his hopes had been raised by the birds apparently pairing up and entering the nest-box, where "the hen would sit for hours on end, but on going in to investigate her only interest seemed to be biting the box to pieces. These birds live amicably during nine months of the year, but the late spring and early summer months they spend their time quarrelling and fighting which assures me they are a true pair..." (Furner, 1936).

Here was someone who was convinced that if two birds quarrelled they must be male and female! I suspect that they were two males. A fit, mature female will almost certainly lay eggs sooner or later.

Young birds

If two young caiques are purchased it is best to obtain them at the same time, but not from the same breeder unless he or she can provide unrelated birds. Caiques like to roost in a nest-box. The problem with this is that its presence might stimulate them to breed before the female is sufficiently mature. Although females might lay earlier, it is not advisable to permit them to breed before their third year. This might not achieve anything, anyway, as young females might lay only a single egg that will probably be infertile. They might be too immature to incubate properly and a habit of egg-breaking could develop. As a matter of fact, caiques can treat their eggs very roughly. A friend who used a nest-box camera was horrified to discover what went on in the nest-box – yet the eggs hatched!

Nest-boxes

The nest-box size is not crucial to success; an important factor is the size of the entrance hole. It should be only just large enough to admit the birds, that is, about 2 1/2 in (6cm) in diameter. A suitable size nest-box might be 18in (45cm) to 2ft 6in (75cm) high with a base 10in (25cm) square. Alternatively, some breeders prefer to offer horizontal nest-boxes, measuring about 2ft (61cm) long and 10in (25cm) wide and high. An inspection door should be made in the back of the box, about 2in (5cm) above the base. If nest inspection must occur (unwisely) from inside an aviary, the inspection door would have to be in the front or side of the box, to prevent taking it down.

To withstand the destructive beak of the caique, the box should be made of wood, such as marine ply, about 1in (2.5cm) thick, with the base of double thickness. Under no circumstances should metal or other unnatural materials be used for the nest site. They provide no insulation and will be hot in summer and cold in winter; they do not "breathe" like wood and they retain moisture.

12. *P. l. xanthomeria* chick, the first area to feather is the wing

13. *P. l. xanthomeria*; the same chick 15 days later

14. *P. l. xanthomeria* aged days 17 weeks, hatched at Loro Parque

15. The three Yellow-thighed Caiques illustrated as chicks at nine months old

16.,17.,18. Young Yellow-thighed Caiques showing different amounts of pigment on bare skin around the eye

19. Family of Yellow-thighed Caiques; note the yellow breasts of the young

20. Aviaries for caiques and other small neotropical parrots at Plantaria bird park in Germany

For caiques, with their innate need to gnaw, they would be uncomfortable and unstimulating.

The life of the nest-box will be prolonged if offcuts of wood are screwed to the inside of the box. Failure to do this will result in the necessity to construct a new box at least once a year. The bottom can be packed with wood shavings to a depth of 2in (5cm) or more. Alternatively, if enough offcuts are screwed inside, the caiques will produce their own nesting material. Gnawing probably stimulates them to breed and is certainly helpful in preventing overgrown beaks.

Caiques (like conures) are not suspicious of a new nest-box. They usually behave as though they cannot wait to enter! Holes entice them. Whirring the wings and whistling in excitement, a new box will usually be explored almost immediately. The nest-box should be placed on the outside of the breeding cage, for ease of inspection and to prevent undue disturbance. Likewise in an aviary, it is not advisable to have to enter the flight when the birds are breeding, because caiques can be very aggressive.

Breeding season

In northern Europe, caiques kept in outdoor aviaries usually start to breed in April or May. Those kept under artificial light with some heat will start much earlier. Indeed, some pairs might nest at any time of year. When breeding seems imminent, it is advisable to add a calcium additive to the food, a powdered additive that can be sprinkled *very* lightly on fruit or softfood. If the female's diet is deficient in calcium she will absorb calcium from her own bones, in order to form eggshells, and this could result in her becoming lame or paralysed. The supplement should be continued until the chicks fledge or are removed for hand-rearing as chicks must have sufficient calcium for good bone growth. If this is lacking in the diet, young will suffer from rickets and will be permanently crippled or must be destroyed.

Breeding will be initiated by the male swaggering along the perch, with blazing eyes, in pursuit of the female. One breeder described her pair in breeding condition as follows:

"During March, April, May and early June my Caiques made mating as much a part of their daily activities as bathing and eating. During this period both birds' plumage intensified and the feather texture of their creamy vests and bright orange trousers turned woolly. The cock in particular took to strutting about in a quite absurd fashion, continually flaunting himself in front of the Sonorans (White-fronted Amazons) in the adjoining aviary, so much so that they changed their perching position to the opposite side" (Uebele, 1983).

At this time the person doing the feeding needs to take great care because the male might also come at him or her (still with blazing eyes!) intent on biting! If the female accepts the food the male regurgitates for her, mating should follow soon after. If the female is not receptive she will move away from the male, or even ward him off using a foot! Or she might duck down under the perch. If she is receptive, he will place one foot on the female's back and keep the other on the perch during copulation, in the manner of most neotropical parrots. Pairs mate frequently prior to egg-laying and copulation can last for several minutes.

A compatible pair keeps close together, usually so close as to be in physical contact, and much mutual preening occurs. The female will spend increasingly long periods in the nest for a couple of weeks before she lays. The clutch size is usually three but clutches of two or four are not uncommon. Mrs Uebele described the "plaintive, almost human crying" made by the female before she laid an egg. This only ceased when the male entered the nest.

A caique egg weighs about 9g. Eggs measure in the region of 32 × 24mm. For example, one captive Yellow-thighed female's eggs measured 32.5 × 24.7mm and 33.7 × 23.6mm (Mann, 1976).

Two eggs of a wild female were measured at 31 × 25mm and 30 × 25mm.

The interval between eggs is usually three days but eggs might be laid every other day. Incubation usually commences when the first or second egg is laid or, more rarely, not until the clutch is complete. Each egg is incubated for about 25 days but the first egg might not hatch until 28 days after it was laid. In warm weather the incubation period could be shorter. For example, in the UK Bob Mann recorded that the first of three eggs was laid by his Yellow-thighed Caique on July 30. The weather throughout was exceptionally warm. The first chick hatched on or by August 23, a second on the 26th and the third on the 29th. As the chicks hatched at three-day intervals the eggs were almost certainly laid at the same interval, giving a 24-day incubation period for each egg (Mann, 1976).

Only the female incubates although the male might spend long periods in the nest-box with the female during the day. He also roosts there at night. Some, if not all, males, take an enormous interest in the events inside the nest-box. A friend related what happened when her young pair of Black-headed Caiques bred for the first time. Soon after the female laid the male was seen to be missing the feathers of his thighs, so that they looked like "bare drumsticks". This puzzled her, as there were no feathers under the cage. When she looked inside the nest-box she found that he had used his feathers as a soft bed for the eggs! This showed not only great concern on the part of the male but intelligent thinking. It will be interesting to see if he repeats the behaviour when the next clutch of eggs is laid. Their first clutch produced one parent-reared youngster.

When chicks hatch

While incubating the female is fed by the male. George Smith observed:

"The feeding bird firmly grasps the upper beak of the recipient at right angles and the food is pushed, by the tongue, into the side of the bill... Feeding in this side-beak 'conure fashion' seems to be more messy than the 'orthodox' way for the hen very soon acquires a dirty face from spillage and, following each feeding, portions of the meal can be seen adhering to the upper mandible."

The sound she makes to solicit food from the male might be mistaken for the food soliciting cries of a young chick. If four chicks hatch the youngest is unlikely to survive, and might not even be fed. Because chicks hatch at intervals of two or three days, the size discrepancy between the oldest and the youngest chick is so great that the stronger chicks will take all the food. The fourth chick usually dies at about two days old but, on rare occasions, has lived as long as nine or ten days in the nest. This problem can be overcome by removing the first chick from the nest at about a week old or when the fourth hatches and hand-feeding it. The older chick could be returned to the nest later if the youngest is large enough to demand its share of the food.

Newly hatched caiques usually weigh about 7g or 8g; weights as low as 5g have been recorded. On hatching they are pink and almost naked, possessing a minimal amount of down. The bill is without pigment; it has a prominent fleshy pad on each side of the upper mandible. As chicks grow these pads gradually become less noticeable. By about the age of three days the down has worn off, and the chick looks quite pink and shiny. By about 18 days the eyes have started to open and a small amount of second down is starting to grow. As caiques inhabit lowland tropical areas, the chicks acquire only a small amount of down, unlike neotropical species from mountainous or sub-tropical areas. At the time the eyes open, closed ringing can take place. The correct size ring is 8.5mm (British size T). At the age of five (or, perhaps, six) weeks the contour feathers are erupting.

George Smith, who was the first to produce a pure-bred caique in Britain, a Black-headed, recorded the development of this parent-reared chick as follows: 18 days, no trace of feathers; 27 days, beak darkening; 29 days, eyes open, feet and beak fairly dark; 36 days, quills on wings and crown prominent.

Weights were as follows:
32 days – 97g; 33 days – 100g; 38 days – 111g; 39 days – 115g; · 41 days – 120g; 43 days – 125g; 46 days – 126g; 54 days – 137g; 73 days (left nest) – 124g.

It is desirable to check the chicks in the nest frequently to ensure that all is well. However, frequency of nest inspection will depend on the reaction of the pair. Some are so aggressive in defence of the nest and young that it is a mistake to try to inspect the nest when a parent is inside. These aggressive birds will attack the intruding hand.

Special attention must be paid to the food. Caiques cannot be expected to rear on only seed or pellets, and fruit. They need a soft nutritious food, containing protein, offered fresh about three times daily (see Chapter 4). Offering small amounts several times daily stimulates the parents to feed their young. It also prevents the food becoming sour or drying up in warm weather. Ensure that clean water is available at all times as caiques drink more when rearing. Some dunk food in their water! When incubating, the female might bathe to achieve the correct humidity in the nest.

Parent-reared young usually fledge at 65 to 75 days, with 70 days being the usual age. The young ones spend several days looking out of the nest before they emerge. They might stay out for only a few minutes at first, venturing out for gradually longer periods each day.

A female might lay again ten to 14 days after the young have fledged. If there is only a single young one it can be left with the parents while the next nest of young are reared. This could be valuable experience for a bird whose future is for breeding purposes. If more than one youngster has fledged and the female is incubating again, it is advisable to remove the young as soon as they are independent – probably four weeks after leaving the nest – because their presence in the nest-box could cause rearing failure.

I believe that every pair of caiques should have an opportunity to rear young, even if only one chick is left with them each year. It must enrich their lives to complete the rearing process, and for eggs or chicks to be routinely removed must be very frustrating for them – the equivalent of every nest being predated. Parent--rearing does not always go smoothly, however.

Breeding sagas

As an example, I will chronicle two breeding seasons of a pair of Yellow-thighed Caiques at Loro Parque, Tenerife. The pair was on exhibit in a busy section of the park. In a quieter environment the results might have been very different. The first of four fertile eggs was laid on or by April 23. The first chick hatched on May 20 and the second on May 21. By May 28 there were four chicks in the nest. Three of these had died by June 8 when the survivor was removed for hand-rearing.

The female did not lay again until the end of December. On January 20 there were three chicks in the nest. The fourth had hatched by January 22. On the 29th two chicks were removed for hand-rearing, weighing 21.8g (at nine days) and 17.4g (at seven days). Note that the fourth survived more than one week in the nest. On January 31st it was found dead in the nest. Its wings had been bitten and there was a large bruise on its head. Had this chick been attacked as the result of interference (the removal of two chicks)? The surviving chick, aged 11 days but weighing only 19.3g, was then removed to join its siblings in the hand-rearing room.

The female laid the first egg of the next clutch on March 7. One chick had hatched by April 5, the second on April 6 and the third by the 12th. The third chick died the following day.

These days, sadly, few caiques have the opportunity to rear a nest of young. An early breeder in the UK was Mr J. Machin of Lincoln. His Black-headed pair was obtained in 1978 and had been imported at least four years previously. In the spring of 1980 the male started to feed the female and mating occurred, usually several times daily. By May the female was spending long periods inside the nest and the sound of splintering wood could be heard. The first egg was laid on June 9, after which the female made an almost continuous plaintive call from inside the nest. Three eggs were laid, on alternate days. The first chick hatched after 28 days; two more hatched but one died at about eight days.

The parents were "ravenous feeders" while the young were in the nest, taking soaked seeds, apple, and bread and milk. Orange, a former favourite, was refused until after the chicks fledged, during the last week in September. The young were very nervous and would retire to the nest-box or crash about the aviary like young grass parakeets. Sadly, one was found dead in the flight, apparently with a broken neck. Adult plumage of the surviving bird was acquired at about 12 months.

The pair then bred every year except in 1983 when, on the suggestion of another breeder, the pair was moved to an indoor flight. A number of fertile eggs were laid, but none hatched. The pair commenced breeding when moved back to their outdoor aviary in 1984. A male from this pair that hatched in 1981 fertilised eggs (with an older hen) in 1983 (Machin, pers. comm., 1986).

Breeding in a group

Male caiques are more aggressive than females so one might surmise that although a trio consisting of two females and one male could live together and breed, the outcome would be very different if there were more than two adult males in a group. Mike Gammond, curator of a large private bird collection in Bahrain, related an interesting story about five wild-caught Black-headed Caiques that he acquired. They turned out to be four males and one female. When they matured one of the males was attacked by the others and was removed. Two males and the only female were left together and bred successfully. One of the young females produced paired with one of the males when she was two years old and was incubating at the time this was related to me. This did not occur in a large aviary but in one only 6ft (1.8m) square and 6ft high!

Breeding hybrids

"Hybrid" is the term given to the young produced from pairing two distinct species or sub-species. It is considered unethical to produce hybrids as it could result in pure stock being lost to aviculture.

An early British breeding of caiques occurred between a male Black-headed and a female White-bellied kept by Lady Poltimore. They were described as tame and delightful, especially the female. The male became "very savage" during the breeding season. For one year they were kept in a cage and let out daily to fly around the room but Lady Poltimore felt that such active birds should have more freedom and exercise. In the summer of 1932 they were placed in an outdoor aviary, the indoor part of which was heated with hot water pipes. It had a large "garden flight" – but the pair was always shut inside at night. They were described as being "very susceptible to cold" and, when they bred that summer, they had artificial heat at times.

The female had laid infertile eggs during the previous two years. That year they started to nest in May, when four eggs were laid. During the incubation period, the male sat on the perch outside, ready to attack anyone who ventured too near his nest. Both the gardeners who fed them had been badly bitten by him on many occasions. Four chicks hatched. A few days later when the nest was inspected again the two smallest chicks had died; it was suspected that they had not been fed. Three weeks later it was found that one of the chicks was twice the size of the other, as the larger one appeared to be receiving most of the food. It was thought that the male was doing most of the feeding. The younger chick died at about six weeks old. It resembled the female in plumage but was very small. The other one left the nest at two and a half months old, when it was as large as its parents and strong on the wing. It had looked out of the nest entrance for a long time before emerging. When it did emerge, it would scuttle back to the nest if anything alarmed it.

When the breeding was reported, it was feeding itself on soaked biscuit, soaked sunflower seed and fruit, and had just started to eat small pieces of walnut. The rearing food had consisted of those items plus oats, the usual seed mixture and mealworms. They ate mainly soaked biscuit and soaked sunflower. Fruit offered was pears, grapes, oranges and apples. They were very fond of walnuts.

The young bird looked exactly like the Black-headed parent except that his thighs were green, like those of the female, and there was more salmon colour at the back of his neck. His pugnacious behaviour suggested that he was a male. He had been seen to attack the female when she was feeding from the same dish. Very tame, he allowed himself to be picked up by people he knew, but was afraid of strangers (Poltimore, 1936).

It is interesting that the young produced in this case showed characteristics of both parents in their plumage. However, if two yellow-thighed forms were paired together, it might be difficult to know that the resulting young were bred from parents with different coloration.

57/

Twenty-two years later, Lady Poltimore reported again on this pair. By this time she was living in southern Rhodesia (now Zimbabwe). The female laid every winter (sometimes two clutches) but the eggs were removed at once because on the occasion when the two chicks hatched "the little hen nearly died". In actual fact, Lady Poltimore could have damaged the female's health by removing the eggs so quickly. To prevent caiques (and other parrots) breeding, they should not be prevented from laying or have the eggs removed at once. The latter action could cause large clutches of eggs to be laid, depleting the female's calcium reserves. The best course of action is to replace the new-laid eggs with infertile eggs from other birds, or with dummy eggs, and to let her incubate these. This is also less frustrating for the pair than to have their eggs removed immediately.

Lady Poltimore reported that the young bird lived only two years. It had to be separated from its parents as it caused disharmony by trying to mate with its mother (Poltimore, 1958).

In the UK in 1971 Frank Wait of Suffolk reared a similar hybrid. A female White-bellied lived peacefully with the pair and was allowed to enter the nest-box. At Busch Gardens, Tampa, Florida, a *leucogaster* × *xanthomeria* pair (already mentioned) had produced nine young by 1969. They all lived together! In a photograph I took in the early 1980s the thigh colour of only one bird could be distinguished. It was lime green!

Chapter 7

Hand-rearing

It is unfortunate that consumers expect parrots for the pet trade to have been hand-reared. In the case of caiques this is unnecessary, as any sympathetic person with a little patience can quickly tame a young parent-reared caique, removed from its parents as soon as it is independent. They are very amenable to taming – unlike some parent-reared parrots.

Where caiques are concerned, hand-rearing is very useful to save younger chicks in large nests. It appears that caiques are not capable of rearing four chicks to independence. As already explained, the youngest of four (or even of three) will usually die soon after hatching or before the age of ten days. The best ploy is to remove the oldest chick or the two older ones, to give the younger ones a chance. A very experienced hand-feeder could remove the youngest chick or chicks.

An inexperienced person would be advised to follow these guidelines:

1. You have at least four years' experience in bird breeding. It does not matter in which species except that they should be altricial, ie, those hatched blind and naked. This gives you the experience of knowing what a normal, healthy chick looks like.

2. You and/or another member of your household are available to give round-the clock feeds or with a break of seven or eight hours. (In some cases this has meant taking chicks to work in a specially adapted cage or brooder!)

3. You must be committed to looking after this chick or chicks for four months. You realise that it is unethical to sell unweaned chicks.

4. You do not rear from the egg if you have not hand-reared parrots before.

5. You have unlimited patience.

6. The importance of good hygiene is firmly instilled in your mind.

7. You should obtain a book and/or a video on hand-rearing. Do not read it or watch it only once; do so three or four times until you are thoroughly familiar with the contents.

Temperature control

The first requirement is a reliable brooder. These are expensive because accurate temperature control is imperative. More chicks die of overheating than due to a temperature that is too low. The latter is obvious because chicks would be lethargic, feel cool to the touch and food digestion would be slow. A chick that is too hot might be extremely restless. Incubator-hatched chicks should be maintained at the same temperature as the incubator for the first few days. Two good quality thermometers should be used to warn if one is faulty. Caique chicks have virtually no down; before their feathers erupt they can be maintained at a temperature between 90–95 deg °F (32–35 deg °C) depending on whether or not there are other chicks to keep them warm, and on the requirements of individual chicks. A single chick will usually require more heat than several, which will cluster together.

The longer you leave a chick in the nest, up until the time its eyes open, the easier it should be for you to rear. Small chicks are difficult for people with large hands to handle. Unfeathered chicks must be handled gently with warm hands; very small chicks should be wrapped in a tissue while outside the brooder to prevent heat loss. Humidity is also important. Keep a small spill--proof container of water, to which chicks cannot gain access, in the brooder.

A single chick needs support. A common mistake of the beginner is to put a small chick in a container with nothing around it. Put it in a small container and pack tissues around it. The popular notion that hygiene is maintained by placing chicks in individual containers should be ignored. If disease is present it will spread anyway, on your hands or clothes, or on the feeding implements if these are not cleaned after each chick is fed. Without its parents, a chick needs physical contact with another chick. It does not matter if this is a different species or slightly larger, it will fare better with a companion.

Methods of feeding

The easiest implement for feeding small chicks is a teaspoon with the sides bent inwards. If you have never fed a chick before, do not try to feed into the crop. It is easy for an inexperienced person to kill a chick. In the wrong hands, the tube can go into the windpipe instead of into the crop. Although it is possible to aspirate a chick using a spoon, this is extremely unlikely. An enormous danger in syringe-feeding into the crop, using a tube or a crop needle, is that the food is too hot. This has often resulted in excruciatingly painful crop burns and death.

A chick will feed readily from the spoon from the day it is hatched – provided that the spoon is warm. Test the temperature of the spoon and the food on the inside of your wrist. At first use a thermometer to test the food. It should be fed at about 109 deg °F (42.7 deg °C) for very young chicks, gradually reducing to 104 deg °F (40 deg °C) for older chicks. The spoon must be warm but not too hot.

Some people prefer to use a 3ml plastic syringe for small chicks, feeding into the beak. Another implement that can be used is a medical pipette. All these instruments must be washed after each chick is fed, or use a whole bowl of syringes, one per chick.

One great advantage of spoon-feeding, or syringe-feeding into the mouth, is that if the food is too hot (or too cold), the chick will shake its head and refuse it. When it is older, it will also do this when it has had enough. (This often makes weaning easier as you are not giving a chick more than it wants to take.)

If you are feeding several chicks, the food will cool before you have fed them all. Start with the youngest, as older chicks do not need food quite so warm. If they are all the same age, or if there are more than one clutch of chicks, you can stand the container of hot food in a bowl of boiling water to help to maintain its temperature. You could reheat the food – but not more than once. Take great care in using a microwave to heat food (not recommended). There could be hot spots in the food, resulting in a crop burn.

Rearing food

The food you give to newly hatched chicks should be diluted for the first couple of days with an electrolyte solution. In the UK chemists sell small sachets of electrolytes in powder form, used to hydrate babies suffering from diarrhoea. An electrolyte solution restores fluids and minerals to the system and is especially good for incubator-hatched chicks, many of which are dehydrated on hatching. The electrolyte solution widely used by parrot breeders in the USA is *Pedialyte*, made by *Ross Products Division of Abbott Laboratories*.

Some people have had problems in rearing caiques from the egg. Certainly losses have occurred when the chicks are fed on certain hand-feeding formulas. They seem to be too difficult for them to digest. I would recommend adding at least 10% fruit to the food, either ripe papaya or tinned strained baby food (fruit-

-based). George Smith adds not fruit but frozen peas to his rearing food. Success in rearing from the egg has been obtained by several breeders using the well-known *Kay-tee Exact*, specifically that formulated for macaws, because the higher fat content seems to suit caiques better. One breeder adds *Vetark's Avipro* (probiotic) to a very diluted formula for the first couple of days, having formerly used Paediatric Avipro (no longer available). Another includes an American product, *Avico Lory Life Nectar Powder*, in the food, also a pinch of powdered garlic – a natural antibiotic.

One breeder of Yellow-thighed Caiques had very poor results when using a lesser-known British brand of hand-rearing food. The chicks hardly gained weight. Within two days of changing to *Kay-tee Exact* they had almost doubled their size and then grew without problems. Due to the early setback they were not weaned until the age of 16 to 18 weeks.

An American breeder who rears chicks from the egg uses a canned soy formula for human babies mixed with an equal amount of *Pedialyte* for the first few days, before changing to a commercial formula (Weaver, 1995).

Chicks will grow slowly during the first few days if hand-reared, gaining very little weight. However, if the food is being digested well and the chicks seem healthy, there is probably no cause for concern and they will eventually start to make appreciable weight gains. Parent-reared chicks reach adult weight at about five or six weeks old. Hand-reared chicks usually take longer to achieve this weight.

It does not matter how good the food is – a commercially prepared formula or otherwise – if a chick has been poorly fed in the nest during the first few days of its life, it might never make a healthy specimen. In fact, poorly fed parents can produce chicks that are weak from the time they hatch. Make sure that your breeding birds have a nutritious diet and offer a calcium supplement. This is probably best added to a good quality rearing food, or to some favoured food item.

Frequency of feeding

There can be no precise rule on this, as much depends on the food offered. As a general rule, after chicks are three or four days old they will need to be fed every two and a half hours and from the age of about three weeks, every three and a half hours. These guidelines are given on the assumption that chicks are fed just after the crop has emptied and that the crop is not filled to the maximum, an unwise procedure that can result in problems. Commercial breeders often recommend "stretching" the crop (ie, always filling it to the maximum) so that chicks do not need to be fed so frequently. Ignore this advice.

Weighing of young

Weighing of chicks is important as an early-warning system. You need to buy electronic scales that weigh to the nearest gram. Each chick should be weighed before and after the first feed of the day. If several chicks of the same species and similar age are being reared, it is essential to be able to identify them. Closed ringing is the best method. Closed rings should be fitted just before the eyes open. Before chicks are old enough to ring, they might be identified with a felt-tipped pen. Weighing of young chicks will be pointless if the scales do not weigh to the nearest gram. Weights should immediately be entered on a data sheet. These should show gradual increases until the age of about six weeks. Then their weight is stable, and starts to decline as fledging approaches. Failure to gain weight indicates a problem, usually a bacterial, viral or candida infection. Seek veterinary advice as only a vet can carry out the tests to identify the problem.

The growth of chicks should be carefully observed for any abnormalities or weaknesses in the legs, wings, spine and beak. A vet should be consulted immediately to advise on calcium and Vitamin D supplementation.

21. Yellow-tailed Caique *(P. l. xanthurus)* with Nelson Kawall in Brazil

22. The same Yellow-tailed Caique displaying to a White-bellied Caique

23. Yellow-thighed Caique in Peru, near the Madre de Dios river

24. Black-headed Caiques near Sacha Lodge, Ecuador

25. Nest site of Yellow-thighed Caiques, with one caique leaving the nest on lower branch (same location as previous photo)

26. Foods suitable for caiques at the weaning stage (and for adults): including fresh corn, sweetcorn, pomegranates and wholegrain bread

27. Skins of Black-headed Caiques collected in Venezuela. Top row: from Delta Amacuro (left) and Bolivar; middle row: from Bolivar; bottom row: from Amazonas. Note the different shades of orange

What are your chicks standing on?

One of the most common mistakes made by the newcomer to hand-rearing is not to pay enough attention to the surface on which the chicks are standing. It is not advisable to keep them on tissues or towelling for longer than three weeks. I recommend the use of plastic mesh or plastic covered mesh of a small size, obtainable from a garden centre. Welded mesh (no larger than 1/2 in square) could be used but it is hard on tender feet. Plastic is softer. Make sure that the mesh is not so large it can trap the tiny feet. Mesh should be bent downwards around the edges, to fit the container or brooder, and stand about 1in (2.5cm) above the floor. If the mesh is too close to the floor, chicks will be standing in their own faeces. Do not let chicks have access to wood shavings. They could swallow them with fatal results.

Keeping chicks clean

During feeding, any food that falls on the chick's skin or plumage must be wiped off immediately. A damp piece of paper towel is suitable for this purpose. The chick's beak and, if necessary, the space under the lower mandible, must also be cleaned after the chick has been fed. A cotton bud can be used, if necessary, to wipe inside the lower mandible, to prevent food adhering there. Accumulated food is an ideal medium in which bacteria and fungus *(Candida albicans)* can grow.

Most breeders remove caique chicks for hand-feeding as early as seven to ten days after hatching. In fact they can be left in the nest longer, and will benefit from being fed by their parents for an extended period. On one occasion, I had to remove two Black--headed Caiques from the nest (at Loro Parque) when they were 49 and 51 days old because the range of aviaries in which they were housed was being pulled down. They were a joy to rear from this age, when they weighed 143g and 129g.

If the young are to be closed-ringed this should occur at the time the eyes start to open, at about 17 days. The ring size is 8.5mm (British size M). At this time the second down, sparse and whitish, starts to grow. At about four weeks the contour feathers appear. Peak weights of chicks I hand-reared were between 150g and 160g and weaning weights were in the region of 145g to 150g.

Weaning

The usual weaning age of hand-reared young is 13 to 14 weeks although I was quite happy to feed certain youngsters until they were 16 weeks old if they needed this. The age varies according to the circumstances. A single chick usually takes longer to wean, as do those with early rearing setbacks. From the age of about seven weeks young can be offered soft items to nibble at, such as wholegrain bread, orange and warm, cooked peas. At first they will consume little. As they start to consume some, other items can be offered, such as spray millet and ripe pear. A softfood can be made up in a food mixer, using wholegrain bread, hard-boiled egg and carrot as the base, and adding a little fruit. Mixed to a crumbly (not wet) consistency it is ideal for young birds. Young caiques are often attracted to brightly coloured foods, such as red pepper, carrot and orange.

A common mistake on the part of the feeder is to reduce the number of feeds too quickly. When the young caiques start to feed on their own, it is the amount of food given at each feed that should be reduced. If a young parrot is hungry, it will be miserable and cry to be fed. If it has been fed and its crop is half full, it will feel contented and will start to nibble at food.

One breeder stated that weaning weights of Black-headed Caiques were 120g to 135g and that the young were easily weaned on to an extruded diet or on to seed at 12 to 14 weeks. I would consider these weaning weights to be low. The practice of weaning young parrots on to hard foods at an early age is to be deplored and can result in early death. If they are to thrive and not to lose too much weight, they must be weaned on to soft foods. Fresh corn on the cob is the favoured food and this and other soft foods as the main part of the diet should be available for weeks after hand-feeding ceases. They will choose to take very little hard seed, pellets or extruded food if soft items of food are available. In the wild, young caiques would be fed for some weeks by their parents, and would only gradually start to feed themselves, almost certainly commencing with the softer food items.

Caiques stay together in family groups for many months, and roost together at night. A single caique needs the contact of another young parrot for companionship and play. But beware of placing a young parrot of another species with several caiques! It might be bullied or even injured. Even before they are weaned, young caiques are very bold and adventurous. One friend told me that three young Black-headed Caiques that he was hand-rearing intimidated his two small dogs to the degree that they would run out of the room!

When the caiques you have reared go to a new home, their weights should have been stable or increasing for a couple of weeks, and they will perhaps still be on one feed per day. Ensure that the new owner knows how to continue this hand-feeding and supply him or her with some of the rearing food. Many parrots suffer weaning regression when they go to a new home. They start off by being hungry and anxious and, as a result, might never fulfil their potential as wonderful pets.

Chapter 8

Health Care

The aim of those who care for caiques should be to prevent ill health. It is indeed true that prevention is better than cure – and much easier. Poor health can be prevented and is unlikely to occur if the following rules are followed.

➤ Offer a diet that is balanced and healthy. Fortunately, caiques readily sample a wide range of foods so the main factor is to get the balance right and ensure that the diet contains at least 40% fresh fruits and vegetables.

➤ Do not try to economise by buying poor quality food.

➤ Maintain a high standard of cleanliness for cages, aviaries and food and water containers.

➤ Prevent access to items containing lead and zinc and other toxic elements.

➤ Do not expose birds kept outdoors to harsh weather conditions from which they cannot escape.

➤ Check birds in outside aviaries at least twice daily – at first light and before they roost.

➤ Physically examine each bird twice a year. Always pay attention to beak and nails. If it is ringed (banded) check that the ring is in good condition and that the leg beneath the ring is not swollen.

➤ **Avoid situations that cause stress.**

Recognising a sick bird

Any change in your bird's normal behaviour and/or vocalisations might indicate it is sick, so observe your caique carefully at all times. Note its normal food intake and the usual appearance of its droppings. If it is unusually quiet, sleeping more than normal and eating less, it is either ill or suffering from shock. A sick bird sits with ruffled feathers and in a sleeping position but with *both* feet on the perch. Very young or very old birds also sleep with both feet anchored. Healthy birds pull one foot up into the breast feathers, to conserve heat loss.

In the early stages of illness, sick birds close their eyes more often than usual. Their eyes might look dull or sunken, especially if they are dehydrated. Note that dehydration is the biggest enemy of sick birds and can cause their death. It is for this reason that a vet should be contacted immediately a bird becomes ill because he or she can administer rehydrating fluids. The disadvantage of taking it to a vet is that it must be moved out of its normal environment. Keep it warm during the journey and cover the cage or carrier with a blanket. Take a small towel with you to remove the caique from the box or cage.

As a precaution, buy a ceramic infra-red lamp. Sick birds eat little, therefore they cannot maintain their body temperature and fluff out the body feathers to try to trap the air around them. A ceramic infra-red lamp gives out no light, only heat. Sick birds need a temperature in the vicinity of 85 deg °F (29 deg °C). An infra-red lamp placed over one side of its cage is the best method of supplying that heat because the bird can move away from the heat source if it desires. This is not possible in a hospital cage.

Note that removing a bird from its normal cage or familiar environment (or mate) can cause stress. If possible, try not to move it except to take it to a vet. Vets will not prescribe medication without seeing the bird.

Consult an avian vet

Remember that it is seldom possible to diagnose disease in a living bird. A description of the symptoms, unless of obvious physical abnormalities, are seldom significant. A vet will need to carry out tests, with a sample of the faeces or blood, or both, to try to determine what is wrong. Blood screening will indicate whether the liver and kidneys are functioning normally. It does not offer a definite diagnosis but it does eliminate certain possible causes of ill health.

If your bird becomes ill, do not try to treat it yourself. If you give it antibiotics, this will invalidate the faecal analysis that the vet would carry out. The faeces are cultured in order to make an antibiogram. This indicates the most effective antibiotics to use. A culture takes several days, perhaps three or four. In the meantime, if the bird is very sick a broad-spectrum antibiotic will probably be prescribed.

As a generalisation, I would say that caiques have fewer health problems than most parrots. This is probably because they are not easily stressed and readily eat healthy foods. The main setbacks encountered are overgrown beak and nails. However, these occurrences are due to bad management. They are easily avoided (see Chapter 3).

Accidents

Caiques are also more susceptible to accidents than most parrots, due to their fearless and inquisitive nature. Those caring for these birds must be vigilant at all times. Remember that toys are a possible source of danger. Some are safe, others present various hazards which can be difficult for even an experienced eye to identify. Take the clapper in a toy bell, for example. In a case known to me a parrot caught its beak in the split loop used to attach the clapper to the bell. Fortunately, it was released unharmed. If this accident had happened when no one was present, the result could have been fatal.

Wild-caught imports

If you have been unwise enough to buy a recently imported wild-caught caique, take it immediately to an avian vet. Have it tested for chlamydiosis (psittacosis, also now called chlamydophilosis). This disease might occur in any parrot (or pigeon or many other bird species) and is something of which everyone should be aware. Many parrots and Budgerigars are infected but the disease remains latent and is not a problem. In times of stress, such as capture and export, it is activated. Symptoms include respiratory problems, discharge from the eyes or nostrils, poor appetite, soft droppings or just looking off-colour. (Of course these symptoms relate to many other diseases as well.) A single test for this disease is not always accurate because the bird might not be shedding the agent when tested. Treatment, under a vet, consists of medication added to the food or a weekly injection. Both treatments cover a period of 45 days.

Newly imported birds should also be tested for all the viral diseases for which testing is available. It is essential to quarantine them away from your other birds. In Europe, sadly, many wild-caught parrots are imported from Guyana, including Black-headed Caiques. Because birds are held in unhygienic conditions, and crowded ones causing stress, prior to export, few will escape these places disease-free. Aspergillosis is not uncommon in wild-caught caiques, due to poor diet (lack of Vitamin A) and stress. If the bird's breathing is laboured or noisy, suspect aspergillosis which, by this stage, will almost certainly be fatal.

In the sad event of death, remember that if your bird is insured for this, a post mortem report will be necessary to make a claim. This could be carried out by a vet or by an avian diagnostic laboratory.

Chapter 9

In the Wild

Caiques are parrots of the Amazon region. They live in forest canopy where they climb around in search of food. Flight is not as strong as that of most small parrots, a clue to which is provided by the dumpy body shape. It is maintained over small distances. After watching Yellow-thighed Caiques in Peru, Lars Lepperhoff told me: "I could hear quite clearly the sound from their wings when they flew near to the observation tower. They fly quite slowly and look like white balls in the air."

Caiques are not fast enough on their short wings to escape predators by flying any distance and probably dive into thick foliage to keep out of harm's way. Because of the type of habitat in which they evolved – dense forest – and their non-specialist frugivorous diet, they have no need to fly long distances. Their nests are located high in tall trees.

Unlike Amazon parrots, conures and macaws, caiques do not occur in large flocks but in relatively small groups. One of the earliest observers to record his observations was J. Stolzmann who watched them in Peru in the 1870s. He observed that when a group was feeding, they placed a sentinel high in a tree. Since that time, very little has been recorded about the natural history of caiques – perhaps less than for any other genus of well-known neotropical parrots.

The distribution of caiques is centred on the Equator. The Black-headed, nominate race, occurs from south-eastern Colombia eastwards to north-east Venezuela, the Guyanas and northern Brazil. The sub-species *pallida* is found in southern Colombia, eastern Ecuador (western and eastern Andes) and north-eastern Peru.

In 1889 Count von Berlepsch, a noted German ornithologist (who amassed a skin collection of more than 55,000 specimens, mainly neotropical), wrote of the Black-headed:

"The birds of eastern Peru and eastern Ecuador differ from those of Trinidad (which presumably are to be regarded as types) and Guyana by the much brighter, almost citron-yellow colouring of the hypochondria and tibia, which in the birds from Trinidad and Guyana are more or less orange-red or salmon-coloured. The throats and sides of the head and subcaudal feathers are also more brightly coloured in the birds of the upper Amazon. These should perhaps be separated as *C. melanocephala pallida.*"

Count von Berlepsch was a widely respected ornithologist, who had at least two birds named after him, but had he made a mistake in including Trinidad in their distribution? There are places called Trinidad in Peru and Colombia, so confusion might have occurred when looking at the label of a skin. On the other hand, did the Black-headed Caique once occur on Trinidad? It is so close to Venezuela that this is possible. There was suitable habitat and, for example, Blue-headed Pionus are found there. Two years later when Count Salvadori's *Catalogue of the Birds in the British Museum* was published, he made no mention of Trinidad in the range of the Black-headed Caique.

The White-bellied Caique, nominate race, is found only in Brazil, in the northern region from the Rio Madeira to Maranhao. The sub-species *xanthomeria* inhabits eastern Peru and northern Bolivia as far west as western Brazil, south of the Amazon. The distinctive Yellow-tailed Caique, *xanthurus*, is also endemic to Brazil; it occurs south of the Amazon from the Rio Purus and Rio Jurua to the Rio Madeira (Collar, 1997).

Appearance

In captivity caiques bathe often and many birds have snowy-white underparts. White is an unusual colour in parrots (excluding cockatoos), probably because it could make them appear quite conspicuous. In fact, in nature, the underparts of caiques are stained, perhaps from fruits, bark or foliage, and usually have a strong or faint brown tinge. The photograph on the last colour page illustrates this very well.

Wild "hybrids"

A hybrid is the young of a mating between two birds of different species or sub-species so, technically, even if one accepts that all caiques belong to one species, the offspring of any two forms of Caiques are hybrids. Behaviourally and vocally the Black-headed and White-bellied Caiques are identical, thus if their ranges overlapped in the wild, "hybridising" could occur. Novaes (1981) stated that this "was indicated" in a narrow contact zone in the western sector of the range. He based this remark on the appearance of specimens of *leucogaster* from as far east as the Belem district of eastern Para, in northern Brazil. He failed to take into account the fact that juvenile birds have black feathers in the crown!

Habitat

Caiques are essentially birds of lowland forests. The Black-headed might be found up to 3,300ft (1,000m) in the foothills of the Andes. They occur primarily in humid forests but the White--bellied can be found in drier forests in the south of its range. It has been suggested that it possibly prefers forest margins and openings to continuous forest (Collar, 1997). Caiques appear to be sedentary in their habits – not moving far.

Black-headed Caique

Status: Generally common; throughout the extensive range of this species there are some vast areas of intact habitat. Another factor in its advantage is that it favours seasonally flooded forest and such areas are difficult to develop.

Brazil

It is perhaps not well known there. In his 700-page book *Birds in Brazil*, Helmut Sick devotes only five lines to it – description and range only. According to distribution maps, it has a huge range there, covering most of the country north of the Amazon.

Colombia

It is fairly common in humid forests and at forest edges, up to 1,600ft (500m), in the south-eastern part of the country (nominate race), and west and east of the Andes *(pallida)*.

Ecuador

P. m. pallida occurs in forested areas of eastern Ecuador. Some specimens there appear to be intermediate between the nominate race and *pallida*.

Guyana

It is widespread and fairly common. One observer recorded: "I encountered this parrot many times in a small section of sand-belt forest in south-eastern Guyana, visited monthly between 1970 and 1973. Apart from odd sightings of apparently solitary individuals, it was generally seen either in pairs or, quite often, in larger groups of up to five individuals. Observed in each month of the year, no seasonal fluctuations in numbers were detected" (McLoughlin, 1983). It also occurs in French Guiana.

Peru

Common to abundant is its status in the forests of north-eastern Peru. John O'Neill informed me in March 2003: "*Pionites mela-nocephala* and *P. leucogaster* remain common in most of eastern

Peru. They must have been affected by deforestation but they are still seen flying over most areas that are not essentially clear-cut. They are more typically seen zig-zagging between the trees just under the forest canopy, giving their high-pitched squeaky chattering notes. They travel in groups that vary from a pair to a half-dozen or more. These may be family groups."

Surinam

It is common in forests on the coastal sand ridges, in savannah forests and in the extensive forests of the interior (Haverschmidt, 1968).

Venezuela

A fairly common to common resident, it is found in forests of the tropical zone, mainly south of the Orinoco, and in southern Sucre in the north. In this country it is heavily trapped for the domestic pet trade.

White-bellied Caique

Status: Generally common; declining in some areas due to deforestation.

Bolivia

P. l. xanthomeria occurs in north-western Bolivia but is possibly now extinct in the Santa Cruz area (Collar, 1997).

Brazil

The nominate race is found south of the Amazon, from north-western Maranhao and eastern Para to north-eastern Mato Grosso and west to approximately the Madeira region in eastern Amazonas (Forshaw, 1989). The yellow-tailed race, *xanthurus*, occurs only in north-western Brazil from the Machados River on the Rondonia-Amazonas border, on the Purus and Jurua rivers in Amazonas. Birds from the upper Rio Jurua, south-western Amazonas, tend towards *xanthurus* in their coloration. The Yellow-thighed Caique, *xanthomeria*, occurs south of the Amazon in northern Brazil. The species is still common in some areas but must have declined in deforested areas.

Ecuador
It is said by some authors to occur in the eastern part – but this is unsubstantiated and seems to be too far west of its known range.

Peru
P. l. xanthomeria occurs in eastern Peru. In the drier forests in the southern edge of its range, it is unlikely to be as numerous as in humid forests. In Manu National Park, at the Cocha Casha Biological Station, flocks occur in the forest canopy, also in trees in more open country at the margins of lakes. Its density there has been estimated at six pairs per square kilometre.

Breeding

Caiques nest in hollows high in tall trees. The breeding cycle, from mating to fledging of young, takes about 17 weeks. Little has been recorded about their reproduction in the wild and most authors quote aviculturists regarding incubation and fledging periods. It would be nearly impossible to gain this information from wild nests. The reported nesting season varies widely from country to country, but this might be more a reflection on how few nesting reports have been made, than on the true breeding season. Also, this is likely to vary in response to climatic conditions, therefore on the fruiting of the plants on which they rely. For example, the breeding season for Black-headed Caiques is given as October and November in Surinam, as December to February for neighbouring French Guiana, and as April and May for Venezuela and Colombia (Collar, 1997).

In Brazil, a nest of a White-bellied Caique was found in a tree hollow 97ft (30m) high. It contained two eggs (possibly an incomplete clutch). In Guyana, E. McLoughlin was told of a nest of Black-headed Caiques in May 1973. He was taken to the nest about an hour before sunset, and recorded:

> The nest was in a living tree about 70 feet high. The entrance appeared to be a natural, vertical cleft in the main trunk about 55 feet from the ground. The tree was about 20 feet from a trail and about 100 yards from a creek. This was an area of mixed bush and savannah. While I waited in the vicinity of the nest, five birds arrived in a nearby tree and, with the aid of binoculars, these could be identified without difficulty as *P. melanocephala*. Three were noticeably smaller than the others with shorter tails and a noticeably yellow tinge to the somewhat dingy white of their belly feathers.
>
> Many minutes were subsequently spent in a gradual, surreptitious approach to the nest during which time these normally noisy birds were almost completely silent except for a few very soft, subdued sounds, including a clucking "culuck". I was told later of another nest not very far from this one and of several adult *melanocephala* pursued by a hawk, fleeing in different directions. It seemed as if several pairs may have nested within a rather small area (McLoughlin, 1983).

This report is of interest in being almost positive evidence that caiques can rear three young – the reference to three with shorter tails and a yellowish tinge to the underparts. Earlier in the same article McLoughlin referred to groups of up to five, which were almost certainly family groups.

Lars Lepperhoff observed *xanthomeria* in Peru, at Posada, in the Madre de Dios Department near the river of the same name. From an observation platform he watched caiques leaving a hole on the underside of a large branch in a tall tree (Lepperhoff, 2001). It appeared that there was a pair with two young that had already left the nest. On one occasion he saw a swarm of insects enter the nest. Three hours later the insects departed and three caiques were seen at the hole. At Tambopata he observed Yellow-thighed Caiques in bamboo forest and in *Cecropia* trees along the river. Once he saw five birds at the famous clay lick there.

Food sources

A wide range of plants and trees offer fruits, buds, seeds, flowers, nectar and probably pollen, and young leaves on which the caiques feed. In Venezuela, for example, Black-headed Caiques have been recorded (Desenne, 1994) as feeding on the following:

SEEDS	FRUIT PULP	FLOWERS
Pouroma guianensis	*Euterpe precatoria*	*Inga laterifolia*
Oenocarpus bataua	*Clusia grandiflora*	*Eschweilera* species
Hevea benthamiana	*Dialium guianense*	
Caraipa densiflora	*Cynometra hostmanniana*	
Micropholis mensalis	*Micropholis melinoneana*	

In Guyana, McLoughlin was told that they fed on the following:

LOCAL NAME	SCIENTIFIC NAME
Hitia	*Byrsonima coriacea*
Waramia	*Tapirira guianensis*
Poixdoux	*Inga*
Awarra	*Astrocaryum tucumoides*
Cocorite	*Maximilianea regia*
Guava	*Psidium guajava*

The caiques visited farms to feed on cultivated guava and *Inga* fruits. McLoughlin saw a group of five caiques pecking at, and apparently eating, the newly opened yellow-green leaves of a very large deciduous forest tree. Partly eaten leaves were found beneath the tree after the birds had flown. In January 1972 four caiques were observed feeding on the yellow orange pulp/and or the seeds of a tangerine-sized wild fig.

In March 1972 red tubular blossoms were found scattered beneath a tree in which a group of caiques had been feeding. The stalk at the flower base was missing in most cases, although the blossom was intact. McLoughlin had observed several parrot species feeding on flowers.

Insect food

Knowing that the Brown-throated Conure (*Aratinga pertinax*) feeds on termites, McLoughlin gave a piece of termite nest to a captive Black-headed Caique. Eating continually, an estimated 200–300 termites were consumed by the caique in about half an hour. This bird (probably hand-reared) showed a great liking for grasshoppers and small caterpillars.

Roosting

Caiques enter tree holes at night. This habit is not found in parrots that occur in large numbers or in large species, such as Amazons, because there would never be enough cavities. More than any species I know, caiques need to roost in an enclosed space. This is why in a cage they will burrow under the newspaper rather than sleep exposed on a perch. A pet bird needs either a small cloth "bed" or a small wooden box in which to roost.

In eastern Ecuador

In November 2001 I visited eastern Ecuador. From Quito I flew to Coca on the upper Rio Napo, the gateway to the Amazon region. Coca is the popular name for Puerto Francisco de Orellana. Here I boarded a canoe with an outboard motor, for a two and a half hour journey down the Napo. On disembarking, I traversed a boardwalk over the flooded forest for half an hour or so. Then I transferred to a small canoe and glided silently down a narrow creek with a profusion of aquatic vegetation on either side. The canoe took me across an ox-bow lake, and Sacha Lodge came into view. The lodge is set within a 5,000-acre private forest reserve. At first light one morning I walked through the forest to reach a huge kapok tree on a hillside. It emerged above most of the forest giants. Around its trunk was a sturdy wooden staircase of 126 steps, with several small balconies on the way. Soon I was 140ft (43m) up in the canopy. At last I was within the world of the Black-headed Caique.

What a view over the surrounding green sea of trees! The thicker branches are like miniature gardens, loaded with fleshy-leaved, red-flowering bromeliads and other epiphytes. They support many life forms, including tree frogs. After a sudden downpour, the sun came out, lighting up a hundred shades of green, from forest giants to laden fig trees, with the Rio Napo glinting in the distance.

I saw a Yellow-fronted Amazon land in the canopy, its wings momentarily displaying the red speculum. Pairs of Blue-headed Pionus and groups of Weddell's Conures flew overhead. But it was the caiques who made my day! Four of them were feeding and flying around. Often they sat at the top of a tree, exposed against the skyline, their shrill yapping calls echoing through the forest. By chance, my camera caught one bird with wings spread like the mythical Phoenix. At last I was seeing caiques in their true environment. These brief glimpses were so much more satisfying than seeing them in my world. We cannot truly understand a species until we have seen it where it belongs.

Chapter 10

Your Questions Answered

Questions posed by those who keep caiques are often very relevant to others with similar interests. This chapter contains a selection of those queries I have answered during the past three or four years.

FEEDING

➤ *I was giving my Black-headed Caique apple until I saw an item on the internet about apple pips being poisonous to parrots. Is this correct?*
No! Possibly they might be harmful if a caique had several hundred a day – but not in normal quantities. Some of my birds love apple pips and I save them for the birds who relish them most.

➤ *My caiques love walnuts but I recently stopped feeding them when someone told me that walnuts are bad for caiques. Is it true?*
Anything can be harmful if fed to excess. Walnuts have a high fat content and they would be harmful if not rationed. I would suggest that you do not offer more than one walnut per bird per day.

➤ *My one-year-old Black-headed Caique adores hot chilli peppers. Why don't they burn his little tongue?*
This is a very good question, the answer to which has only recently been discovered. Research has revealed that birds, unlike

mammals, lack a protein receptor that responds to capsaicin in the nerve endings on the tongue. Capsaicin is the chemical in peppers that causes mammals to feel a burning sensation when peppers are eaten. This discovery explains why the seeds of peppers are dispersed only by birds.

PETS

➡ *I am considering buying a parrot. The problem is that I recently started to work full time. Can you suggest a suitable species?*

As you are now working full time, you need birds that are capable of amusing themselves. My suggestion to you would be to buy two hand-reared Black-headed Caiques. These little parrots are so entertaining and unlike most parrots, if they are handled daily, a pair will stay tame with you. However, when they mature they could be aggressive (like all parrots) during the breeding season. They play for hours, with each other, and with toys, cardboard boxes, etc. However, they do need fresh cut twigs (apple, for example) on a regular basis to prevent their beaks from becoming overgrown and for rubbing themselves on! Hand-reared young ones are irresistible and in great demand, so you might have to go on to a breeder's waiting list. Do buy them at the same time or within about one month – or jealousy would be a problem. I cannot think of another species that would suit your situation so well.

➡ *I am considering building an aviary so that my caique can play outdoors in fine weather. Is this a good idea?*

Yes! I think your caique would enjoy this very much. I would suggest that you buy lengths of cotton rope and hang these vertically from the roof. Thin rope should be knotted at intervals as a safety measure. You could make some swings using a couple of chains attached to a natural branch, and hung from the roof using key rings. (Chain can be purchased from hardware stores.)

You could also hang a bath from the roof. Obtain a large shallow stainless steel dish, drill three holes in the rim, and buy chain and key rings with which to hang it. No matter how tame he is, do not take any risks by carrying him outside on your hand. Use a small cage.

BREEDING

➽ *My Black-headed Caiques are housed indoors in a cage 3ft (91cm) long, 2ft (61cm) wide and 2ft 6in (75cm) high. There is a nest-box on the side but they throw out all the wood shavings. As far as I know, the female has not laid yet. What can I do to prevent any eggs being broken on the bottom of the box?*

I would suggest that you buy wooden Budgerigar nest-box concaves from a pet shop and fit these into the bottom of the nest-box by cutting wood to fit around the concave so that there is no gap between the concave and the sides of the box. The other alternative is to put fine bird sand in the bottom of the nest, as this will support the eggs. However, some parrots do throw out all the nesting material but this does not necessarily stop them from breeding. If the female lays and there are no wood shavings under the eggs when the clutch is complete, try placing the eggs on a bed of wood shavings, if the female tolerates disturbance. Some females will accept nest material when they have finished laying. I think your cage is much too small for a breeding pair. Such small cages might result in various behaviours that are detrimental to breeding success.

➽ *I bought a proven pair of Yellow-thighed Caiques four months ago. The female has just laid her first egg with me. If chicks hatch I intend to hand-rear them from the egg. Is this difficult and can a commercially-prepared formula be used? Is it necessary to add fruit and, if so, can the fruit be liquidised and frozen in ice cube trays?*

Caiques appear to be difficult to rear from the egg using certain commercial formulas. A formula with a higher fat content, such as one made for macaws, would probably be best. I would strongly recommend that you leave the chicks with the parents for the first ten days. If this is not possible, add some fruit from day one, as this seems to aid digestion of the food. You can either use small jars or tins of fruit baby food, or you can liquidise fruit, preferably ripe papaya. Yes, the thawed liquidised frozen fruit can be used.

➤ *I am returning to parrot keeping after the theft of birds from my outdoor aviaries. I am considering obtaining a pair of Black-headed Caiques as I want to choose a species that can breed without access to an outdoor flight. Will it be necessary to provide them with full--spectrum lighting?*
While this is not absolutely essential, they would certainly benefit from it. Birds kept without access to sunlight or Vitamin D cannot easily assimilate calcium, which could result in breeding problems. Full-spectrum lighting should prevent this happening as it has similar qualities to sunlight. However, continuous exposure to all forms of artificial lighting is not desirable. Try to ensure that the natural lighting in the building is good enough to be able to turn off the lights for a short period during the early afternoon, when the birds are resting. An extra window might be needed. Do not make this in the roof. This could result in the room becoming too hot, it can cause condensation and poses a security risk.

References Cited

Bates, H. J. and R. L. Busenbark, 1959, *Parrots and Related Birds*, T. F. H. Publications, New Jersey.

Bertagnolio, P., 1974, Lories, Lorikeets and Caiques, *Avicultural Magazine*, 80 (6): 238.

Collar. N., 1997, in del Hoyo, J., A. Elliott and J. Sargatal, eds, *Handbook of the Birds of the World*, vol 4, Lynx Edicions, Barcelona.

Dawson, C. R., 1915, Some Colony Birds, *Bird Notes*, New Series, vol III, no 8, 208–210 (reprinted from *Timehri*, May 1915).

Desenne, P., 1994, Estudio Preliminar de la Dieta de 15 Especies de Sitacidos en un Bosque Siempre Verde, 25–41, in Biologia y Conservacion de los Psittacidos de Venezuela, Graficas Giavimar, Caracas.

Friedman, D., 2001, When Rainbow met Kiwi, *Companion Parrot Quarterly*, No 54: 65.

Furner, A. C., 1936, A Derby Member's Aviaries, *Avicultural Magazine*, Fifth Series, 1 (1): 9.

Haverschmidt, F., 1968, *Birds of Surinam*, Oliver and Boyd, Edinburgh.

Hine, B., 1997, Those Caique Clowns, *The Pet Bird Report*, 7 (2): 58–61.

Low, R., 1972, *The Parrots of South America*, John Gifford, London.
1992, *Parrots, their care and breeding*, third (revised) ed, Blandford, London.
1999, *The Loving Care of Pet Parrots*, Hancock House Publishers, Surrey, B. C. and Blaine, Washington.

Mann, R. E. H., 1976, Breeding attempts by White-bellied Caiques, *Avicultural Magazine*, 82 (2): 86–90.

McLoughlin, E., 1983, The Black-headed Caique – field notes, *Avicultural Magazine*, 89 (1): 43–46.

Novaes, F. C., 1981, A estrutura da especie nos periquitos do genero *Pionites* Heine (Psittacidae, Aves), *Bolm Mus. Para Emilio Goeldi*, no 106: 1–21.

Poltimore, Lady, 1936, Breeding of the Black-headed and White-breasted Caiques, *Avicultural Magazine*, Fifth Series (11): 294–296.
1958, Black-headed × White-bellied Caique hybrid and some notes about the wild birds of southern Rhodesia, *Avicultural Magazine*, 64 (3): 89–90.

Prestwich, A. A., 1955, Caiques, *Avicultural Magazine*, 61 (4): 155–167.

Rodriguez-Machecha, J. V. and J. I. Henandez-Camacho, 2002, *Loros de Colombia*, Conservacion Internacional, Bogota.

Roet, E. C., D. S. Mack and N. Dupliax, 1981, Psittacines imported by the United States (October 1979–June 1980), *in Conservation of New World Parrots*, ed R. F. Pasquier, Smithsonian Institute/ICBP.

Sick, H., 1993, *Birds in Brazil*, Princeton University Press, New Jersey.

Smith, G. A., 1971, Black-headed Caiques (*Pionites melanocephala*), *Avicultural Magazine*, 77 (6): 202–218.
1991, The Caique, *The Magazine of the Parrot Society*, XXV (6): 191–197.
1996, The Caiques, *Caged Bird Hobbyist*, 4 (5): 22–25.

Tyson, D., 2003, Life with one, two, three caiques, *Companion Parrot Quarterly*, No 59, 38–42.

Uebele, D., 1983, In Praise of Caiques, *Magazine of the Parrot Society*, XVII (12): 359–364.

Weaver, N. S, 1995, Having fun breeding the Black-headed Caique, *Bird Breeder* 67 (2): 16–19.

Further reading in the German literature:

Brockner, A., 1992, Der Grunzugelpapagei, *Papageien*, 5 (3): 82–84.

Freyer, M., 1996, Erfahrungen mit Grunzugelpapageien, *Papageien*, 9 (10): 294–297.

Lepperhoff, L., 2001, Gelbschenkel-Rostkappenpapageien im Regenwald Westamazoniens, *GefiederteWelt*, 125 (4): 114–117.

CAIQUES

Published, printed and bound in the Czech Republic by
DONA Publishing, Komenského 37, 370 01 České Budějovice.
Photos: R. Low, T. Brosset, L. Lepperhoff, R. Restall.
Design: Jiří Jabulka.

ISBN 80-7322-044-X